UNTAMED EQUALITY
The New Frontier of
Safety, Security and Inclusion

Todd A. Weiler

UNTAMED EQUALITY

The New Frontier of Safety, Security and Inclusion

Todd A. Weiler

For my son, Augustus,
I hope you will live to realize the dreams of
untamed equality.

AUTHOR'S NOTE

This is my first book and it has evolved over the many years of attempts to write it, dating back to my experiences in the Gulf War. I hope that as you read it, you will not find it to be an exercise in the vanity of someone that must be published. It certainly was not an easy task on my part. In addition to the emotional rollercoaster of memories, it presented a challenge in how to tell this story without boring you or upsetting too many people, while keeping it purposeful.

What I have attempted to do in this book is explain the important policies that I believe we must take, particularly in the area of national security. I do this by explaining my life experiences and hopefully paint a picture as to how they shaped my views. The term, *Untamed Equality*, was an idea borne by Candi Cross, who assisted me throughout the writing of this book. My frustration was in articulating a different level of equality...not one that is taught, not one that meets expectations of the majority, but one that is demanded and rightfully so. It is an unconventional term, but one that I have come to embrace.

This book, in many ways, is a national security perspective on social issues and how they all intertwine to create safety and security for us all.

CONTENTS

FOREWORD

"She's with us." A tall, skinny Texan named, Todd Weiler, reached through the surge of Secret Service officers and plucked my wife from the throng. We were kids really. Only, as I'd soon learn, Todd had been to war.

My learning curve was steep that day at University of Colorado Boulder. It was my very first political event and it was a doozy. It was late summer of 1992, Christine and I, in our early twenties, had just gotten married, and Bill Clinton had won the Democratic Nomination for President.

It all happened pretty fast. I was invited to give some opening remarks for Hillary Clinton. Why? Because I'd visited with a publicist at a barbeque in Los Angeles and had acted in a couple of movies. No one checked my credentials. I just said I was eager to participate, and they were looking for support from so-called "young Hollywood." I didn't really have an audience. I was just a passionate citizen, currently studying at Community College.

At that point, Hillary had gone from the completely unknown wife of an obscure southern governor, to an absolute rock star. At this event, just outside of Denver, over 10,000 people had turned up to hear her speak. To the best of my knowledge, it was Hillary's biggest solo event in support of her husband's campaign. Who was in charge of the site? Todd Weiler.

The guy did everything. While I was recognizable to some, I was by no means a top-flight surrogate. That didn't matter. Todd, with the enthusiasm of a teenager, a ready smile and what I would come to know as a distinctly ambitious twinkle in his eye, swooped us up in a campaign rental car and whisked us to the university. He wasn't our planned chauffeur we just happened to land at the motel as he was heading over. I'll never forget that drive. I peppered him with questions and was naively shocked to find out that there was such a thing as a war fighter, who was a Democrat.

Todd's stories blew my mind. His command of the event seemed breezy, even though the stakes were high. How did he know so much about all of this stuff? The media? The campaign? The volunteers? How to manage the crowd? How did he know the way to set the scene, to create the perfect picture for the campaign? How did he know about the physical stage and all of the details that go into fielding such an event? He was so young. And somehow, he had the presence of mind at the moment "the principle" arrived at the location, with the passions of the throng rising, to see that Christine was being shoved into the crowd and effortlessly reach out for her. It may not sound like much, but when Christine playfully but earnestly said, "This guy rescued me," I knew he was special. Special to me, at least. We became fast friends.

For the past thirty years, I have been endlessly amazed at who this man is. Todd's life is a wonder to me. He's from Midland, Texas. I've never seen a flatter place on earth. You can drive through it for days and still not reach the other side. It's remarkable for its endless horizon. But for me, when I think of that lunar landscape, it means something else. Standing at his mother's gravesite, I saw a strong man with a bowed head. *A son.* There was so much she knew about her boy, but so much she didn't.

As with most things in life, we learn about people not from what they say, but from what they do. Reading this is probably the first time Todd will know how much those moments in his hometown meant to me. I'm certain I hugged my mom a little tighter the next time I saw her.

"How would you like to serve as a Civilian Aide to the Secretary of the Army?" That one stopped me in my tracks. I was so proud when Todd was sworn in at the Pentagon. His full title was ridiculous; Deputy Assistant Secretary for Reserve Affairs, Mobilization, Readiness and Training. Every word about Todd's job and his responsibilities were foreign to me. I was a liberal actor from Los Angeles. The incongruity of his question was hard to digest. Why? Why would you ask me this? What is it about our new friendship that gave you the impression I would not embarrass you, the Army, the President, my family...?

What is a civilian aide? Calmly, he explained that the Army did not enjoy a great relationship with young people in the country at that stage. He said, my volunteer job would be to simply learn about the organization and share my experience with others. He possessed absolute confidence in the mission of the Army of the United States and in my ability to learn and share. It turned out to be one of the great privileges of my life to serve in that role for ten years. Todd's instinct was born out. I bonded with the older members of the group and hopefully made some small contribution.

We would go to bases where I met soldiers and their families. I visited with generals and privates and folks up and down the chain of command. And I learned exactly how the Civilian Leadership of our Armed Forces truly works. Todd taught me about service. He led by example. As a government official and a friend, he made me understand what it means to care about soldiers and our national community. He showed me what it means for a military man, not just to want peace, but also to work for it. He helped me draw a straight line from the value of individual lives to the policies that affect them.

All of this high-flying political and governmental work aside, Todd cares about me. When Hurricane Katrina hit, I was despondent. More than outraged at the failure of our country to respond appropriately, to help our citizens in need, I experienced, probably for the first time in my life, true despair. My idealism had been shattered and my faith was shaken to the core. I remember sitting on the patio and looking up. Todd had been in Northern California, on business away from Virginia, and he literally dropped everything to come down to Los Angeles. We'd spent holidays together and countless trips. We'd stayed at each other's houses. We were friends. Very good friends. But this was different. This wasn't about fun and fellowship. This wasn't about careers and our mutual love of civics. This was about one guy knowing that this moment was different. I was crying hard. Todd was there.

As you embark on your journey to know him, I'd suggest that Todd's personal and professional lives fuel each other. As you begin your journey with my friend, understand that his idealism is both true and anchored in reality. Oh, and lest I paint too serious a picture and I'm sure he'd appreciate me saying so, Todd does a wicked impression of Ethel Merman and is quite good at video games. Enjoy!

—*Sean Astin*

INTRODUCTION

IMPACT: THE BURDEN AND BLESSING OF LEADERSHIP

"IF YOUR ACTIONS INSPIRE OTHERS TO DREAM MORE, LEARN MORE, DO MORE AND BECOME MORE, YOU ARE A LEADER."

—JOHN QUINCY ADAMS, U.S. PRESIDENT

Ziauddin Yousafzai, a teacher, was determined to give his daughter every opportunity a boy would have. He operated a girls' school in a village on the outskirts of Mingora, Pakistan. But everything changed when the Taliban took control of the town in scenic Swat Valley, also known as the "Switzerland of Asia" because of its picturesque snowcapped peaks.

The extremists banned television, music and cinema, and enforced harsh punishments for those who defied their orders. Taliban officials established their own courts, announcing and implementing punishment consisting of stonings and beheadings in public places.

Needless to say, when they commanded that girls over the age of 10 could no longer go to school because it was "un-Islamic," most families immediately complied out of fear. Even if they were defiant, there weren't many choices. Within a year, it's estimated that militants blew up or burned 134 schools and colleges, with more than ninety of them being institutions for girls.

In January 2008, when Yousafzai's daughter was just 11 years old, she said goodbye to her classmates, not knowing if she would ever see them again. After all, public life had been dwindled down to a real-life board game of dangers at every corner in the valley. The girl kept a journal about her experiences, but that did not satiate her need to strike out against the injustices accelerating by the day. She wrote a chronicle about Taliban atrocities under a pen name for the BBC's Urdu service, and the world took notice, proclaiming that she was a hero.

In October 2012, a masked gunman boarded a school bus and shot her three times in the head. She woke up ten days later in a hospital in Birmingham, England, and recovered there over the course of months, enduring intense surgeries and rehabilitation. She would never return to Pakistan. By all accounts, that is when her life began.

She said, "It was then I knew I had a choice: I could live a quiet life, or I could make the most of this new life I had been given. I determined to continue my fight until every girl could go to school."

With her father, the teacher, Malala Yousafzai established Malala Fund, a charity dedicated to giving every girl an opportunity to achieve a future she chooses. Malala received the Nobel Peace Prize in December 2014 and became the youngest-ever Nobel laureate. She's studying at the University of Oxford, now...and "fighting every day to ensure all girls receive twelve years of free, safe, quality education."

Her life experience, including surviving an assassination attempt, caused the United Nations to launch a campaign calling for the education of all children worldwide, and eventually led to Pakistan's first Right to Education Bill.

There are watered down versions of *leaders*, and then there are real LEADERS. Today, we see many examples of both. I reference Malala Yousafzai because as a child, a young girl from a part of the world that still, in 2020, rates 153 out of 155 on the World Economic Forum's Gender Gap Index, she demonstrates leadership skills (like speaking up and standing up for a cause) for the *untamed equality* that I am calling for in this book. And if Malala, now 22, can do it, I expect a hell of a lot more figures with greater access, resources, privilege, visibility, and power to as well! The future of our safety, security, and quality of life is at stake, and that is no exaggeration. I speak from my experience as a privileged white male American with a decorated career as a government executive, business owner and combat veteran.

In this book, I hope to explain some directions that I believe the country should follow and the life experiences that led me to these views. Someone (hopefully no one that purchased this book) might say, "What makes him so special to have 'real' plans for this country?" My answer is, I am no one special. However, at the same time, I have come to realize that neither is anyone else. Ideas may be borne by one person, but they are brought to life and implemented by many and therein lies the leadership of which I speak: Leaders motivate. With regard to this book, maybe that is what I am trying to do—motivate you to agree and bring to life these ideas. Perhaps I am hoping that you will see your life experiences driving you to agree with these views, but that is really up to you to decide, so I hope you will read on.

For far too long, I, and I think most Americans, have watched people fill leadership roles yet have no capacity to lead. We see it day in and day out from our jobs to our local government, all the way to Washington, DC. It has become so bad that many Americans believe that most elected leaders are corrupt and those they appoint are worse; from the "yes men" in the President's cabinet, to the local mayor covering for a police department run amuck. And in our careers, we see people placed in leadership roles that, as my mother would say, "couldn't lead one man in an all-girls school". It is true that we are surrounded by people filling leadership roles that are not leaders, but it is also true that there are leaders among us and we are privileged to be living in a moment when these neighborhood, local and even state-level leaders are moving our nation forward during a crisis of abdication from our national leaders. These are the people that have been sidelined for far too long and dismissed as "overly zealous" or "too committed to be effective". Now, we see our national "leaders" running to jump on the bandwagon.

The leaders I speak of and cry out for are those of *untamed equality*. They don't accept the acceptable. They don't take a seat until it is their turn. They don't jump on the bandwagon; they are driving it.

While serving in the Gulf, I learned what the true meaning of altruism is, and not from me or those around me, but from the people back home that would spend their days making baskets and "care packages" or writing endless letters of hope and encouragement. The people that didn't have a direct family member in harm's way, yet would devote so much time, money and effort to making a difference in our lives. That was selfless service. I had seen it before in my mother's life, but I had not truly experienced it since. Now that I saw and felt it as an adult, I can now spot it. It is present as the most prevalent attribute in all my heroes.

In combat, because you think that you might die, you let your guard down and open feelings that were closed off before. I wasn't that close with my fellow pilots; maybe that is because I had been a lieutenant before and was now a warrant officer. They looked at me differently and I looked at them differently. Really, I think it was because I had high aspirations—for instance, still wanting to be President of the United States (more on that later). Yet, most of those around me had dreams of flying helicopters for the Army and then a commercial outfit. That is not a judgement; it is what many of them wanted and I love that, but it was not me. Instead, I spent time with my best friend, a junior enlisted soldier; he had aspirations for great achievements, and I think that connected with me. He also liked my funny nature and talking about the news and politics, so with that going for me, how could I hang out with anyone else? He was my best friend and at that point in the middle of the Iraqi desert, I couldn't imagine life without him.

Some people, many that are close to me, think I can be cold at times and seemingly void of feelings, yet I can cry at the drop of an ASPCA commercial or a child hugging a grandparent. I think it is actually because my emotions have been so refined through experience and loss. Loss of my mother, granddad and grandmother when I was young, but also, through what I saw firsthand in the faces of the people of the Middle East and what I felt as I went to fly my first combat mission and my friends on the ground facing an unknown enemy. It's different to see it and experience it firsthand.

I am full of emotion and empathy, but not for the trivial—it is aroused by the reality of unfair suffering and needless pain. It is aroused in the face of an agonizing death of a parent and the pleading of a grandparent that does not want to be left alone to die. The faces of children in a war zone and the hand of a friend before entering the battle; those raise my emotions. All of this may not make me a great person, but it has certainly shaped who I am: The guy that has no tolerance for the person that constantly shows up late but will walk on coals for the one that has nothing but a dream and a determination.

My time in the Gulf also shaped my professional life. I was a helicopter pilot, so taking chances is what we did. But as a pilot, you analyze and try to balance the risk with the reward. For example, if you are in a Vietnam-era Cobra attack helicopter in the Iraqi Desert and it is 100+ degrees, with a full bag of gas and full armament and you are bouncing the helicopter across the sand just to get enough speed to make it fly, now might not be the time to turn on

the air conditioner (analysis), and if you are successful in your mission, you might save some lives and win the day (reward)!

Certainly, that was a true story. From it, I learned that taking chances can yield great rewards, and there is always a warranted assessment, a calculation that you must make. One of my first missions in Desert Storm was to fly with another Cobra to the western flank of the allied forces entering Iraq. The French forces had met stiff resistance and were unable to break through the Iraqi line. If we could not help them break through, then our left flank would be exposed. *That* is a calculated risk—losing two vital and expensive aircraft (not to mention their crews) for the possibility of breaking the line of the Iraqi defenders and moving the invasion forward.

These moments of many in my short Army career reinforced the importance that I had learned, like most pilots, to always be aware of your surroundings and focus far out in front of the aircraft. This is a lesson that is sometimes lost in the Pentagon, or as many that work inside refer to it as the "five-sided funny farm". You only need to look at the various statutes and policies that guide the vast personnel programs of the 1 million+ member military and its supporting civilians. Many of the statutes were written decades ago and their implementing policies are rarely any newer. We still recruit from storefronts in strip malls, retain based upon programs that were popular in the 1970s and 1980s, and create standards that exclude much of today's society from service and apply the same exact physical requirements on the infantry soldier and the cyber expert.

However, after years of neglect and lower-tier priorities, the department is finally starting to take a closer look at the most important aspect to the readiness of our military, our people. Time will tell whether or not this is a serious effort.

Although the defense department leads in many important advances for our society, like telemedicine and cyber security, we have lagged behind in others, like the culinary arts (ask any veteran) or on a more serious note, gay rights. I experienced this firsthand as the political appointee in the Army that had to implement the Don't Ask Don't Tell policy in the early days of the Clinton Administration. It was a tough pill to swallow and over the years as society progressed and companies created gay-friendly environments, the Department of Defense (DoD) held to this policy until just a few years ago. It could also be said that the department has lagged in opportunities for women, but in each of these cases, we have followed society and now, are removing barriers and creating opportunities. So, where some might say that the military is too often a social experiment, it is actually a mirror of society—a reflection that improves or decays, based on our societal progression, or regression.

As my work in the department focused on tearing down these barriers and creating opportunities, I spoke and continue to speak on the importance of creating a military that is more reflective of our society. I am focused and reassured by those that press equality forward and are never satisfied with what is given or expected. It is this movement forward that makes many uncomfortable yet reassures me that we are on the right path: untamed equality.

New York City developed ninety-six indicators to measure progress toward equality. The United Nations Foundation, sixteen. *The Review of Income and Wealth* refers to "equality of opportunity in four measures of wellbeing." Fortune 500 companies loudly publicize diversity and inclusion (D & I) programs galore. We even have "chief people officers" designed to police equality! Though significant and just, I'm going to call this basket of initiatives and protocol "tamed" equality. Tamed equality is no less valuable and cause for celebration than any other stand *and* demand of equality I will discuss in this book. However, the untamed equality is exactly what we don't have and literally what keeps me up at night. Without it, all other rights are threatened. I am referring to the safety of our people and the security of our nation. It is achieved only through inclusion, for therein lies the strength. It is untamed because it does not follow the rules of "wait your turn" or "let's not dilute our race".

I remember my husband and I attending the Human Rights Campaign (HRC) annual gala in Washington, DC, where I was thrilled and pleasantly surprised by the large number of corporations that were leading the way in LGBTQ rights, not only in their promotion externally, but also, in their corporate policies. I heard from defense companies, aviation and technology leaders that described how they have created policies that went beyond "zero-tolerance" and protections to celebratory actions that promote diversity and gender. My first thought was, *why can't we be more like them*, and then I remembered that it was okay if we, the DoD, didn't always lead the way though followed the good example.

Sometimes change is an iterative process. That is how we become more reflective—that mirror of our society, while preserving the history and structure that makes us the world's greatest fighting force.

What you cannot do, however, is follow in the areas that are important to new recruits. This is the population of our future, where our "money is made". In this area, we must always lead or risk losing large numbers of youth to a more connected, diverse and aware private sector. A willingness to serve goes only so far, when an institution denies entry based upon tattoos, or fails to provide any retirement benefit to those that serve for less than twenty years. I personally led the stalled effort to get a fair retirement system, and I can tell you it was like pulling an abscessed tooth without Novocain.

I am sure that there are those that will accuse me of following the model of molding the military into a social experiment. However, I would simply respond by asking, "Is a military that is reflective of society a social experiment, or is making a military less reflective the social experiment?" This should also be the essence of questions to any nominee to the U.S. Department of Defense. How is it that allowing perfectly willing and able citizens the opportunity to serve their country a social experiment?

In each case that I had the honor of working, opening combat positions to women, fighting for and seeing the removal of Don't Ask, Don't Tell, and implementing the Pentagon's transgender policies, the standard we used was the same. In each case, we took a step away from creating segments of separation and instead, said, "If you want to serve and you can meet the standards, we welcome you into your military."

To me, this is the litmus test that we must always strive to achieve. It is the only standard that will drive us to achieve what I believe we must, a military more reflective of the society we serve. For those that believe we should return to a military of decades ago, I say, "Stop conducting your social experiments on America's Armed Forces."

As of this writing, while sheltering in place, I look at my 18-month-old son and think, *if he only knew!* And he will someday. He'll know that in the year of 2020, his two fathers did their best to secure and protect the family amidst the coronavirus pandemic, one of the most consequential events of our lifetime. I'll tell him, it wasn't without celebration of something as mundane as paper towels! More importantly, he will know about the inequalities that this virus exposed. He will hear how the killing of a black man, George Floyd, led this country to finally face its demons and resolve to change. It is my hope that he won't ever have to face the same dangers, but whether he does or not, I am certain that he will be a LEADER of the next generation.

CHAPTER 1

As the coffee pot spewed its last few drops of water, I filled my cup and proceeded to the den to see what was on the TV. Every morning started the same with a shower, cup of coffee, and then off to work. To my surprise, that morning, the channels were flooded with news of an Iraqi invasion of Kuwait. It seemed that every program was discussing the invasion and the U.S. reaction. Like most Americans and my neighbors, I was taken by surprise. The routine of everyday life was being interrupted with this shocking news.

I had only lived in my Clarksville apartment for three months after moving off post. I moved there because it was close to the Fort Campbell airfield where I worked. My days were like that of most pilots: sit around the conference room telling jokes and stories for a while and then down to the flight line. When I was not on the schedule to fly, I would help work on the aircraft. There wasn't much going on that week. The instructor pilot was on leave for vacation and the rest of us were designated as the Division Ready Force (DRF), which basically means that we couldn't go anywhere because we were the unit that would be deployed first in an emergency. As I made my way to the airfield, I listened to the continuous coverage on the radio. Naturally, everyone had their own opinions, and most were not hesitant about speaking their mind. The reaction at work was what I had expected. "Let's go kick their ass."

In the hours and days that followed, close watch was kept on the Saudis. Would they ask for the U.S. military to protect them from a possible Iraqi invasion? It was becoming all too clear that President Bush had no intention of allowing this invasion of Kuwait to stand unchallenged. The question was whether or not there was a willingness to commit U.S. troops. An unwillingness on behalf of the Saudis to allow U.S. troops on their soil would greatly hinder any plan of military intervention. I don't believe that after the second day of the invasion there was ever a question within the administration about the use of military intervention, at least in so far as the defense of Saudi Arabia. The problem would be in convincing the Saudis of Sadam's serious threat and the need for U.S. assistance.

It took only three days before the groundwork for U.S. troop deployment began. The Saudis had agreed to receive what would be the largest deployment of U.S. troops since World War II. For us, feelings were intense, and this was understandable. We all were still upset that we had not been called to perform the mission in Panama. After all, it was an air assault mission and we, the 101st, were the only air assault division in the world. Many of us felt that we had been left out, and we didn't want to be left out again. Everyone watched and listened to the news in anticipation of our "big chance." Not that we were hoping for a war, but if there was to be one, we wanted to be there.

Plans were made for our deployment and cancelled. Then plans ramped up again and got cancelled. Naturally, this added to the discussion and our frustration; surely, we wouldn't be left out again, after all, we were the 101st! Finally, the order came in that we would deploy to Saudi Arabia. The few individuals that were still on leave were called back and preparations for our deployment began.

What was to follow during the days of preparation could best be described as pandemonium. We soon found ourselves in an intense training program designed to acclimate us to the hot desert environment. This program had a few inherent problems. Ft. Campbell, Kentucky is not what one might consider an arid region; in fact, it is as humid as a greenhouse.

The acclimation training included marches and runs during the heat of the day, in full CPOG (chemical protective over-garment). This provided only a test of exhaustion and did little in preparing for the harsh desert conditions. It *did* provide many of us with our first experience of claustrophobia. The chemical gear, complete with gas mask, completely encases a soldier. Once inside the gear, you begin to feel the rising temperature as the charcoal-lined suit totally inhibits any breeze from cooling your body. The mask also prevents the entrance of cool air and within a matter of minutes, sweat begins to inhibit vision and add to the claustrophobic symptoms. I do not claim to be an expert in this field, but I do know that the idea of having to fight in this suit was not appealing! We would go on marches that became increasingly longer and longer—amid August, so it was about 100 degrees and 100% humidity. By the time we would finish, we would literally pour the water (sweat) out of our boots and gloves. I was just trying not to die during these marches so much so that I had forgotten that I was a bit claustrophobic. (Later, in Saudi Arabia, with Saddam launching SCUD missiles at us, we had to wear the mask for hours at a time and I would be reminded of this condition.)

Soon, the airfield buzzed with activity, as civilian contractors came to place new equipment on board our Vietnam-era Cobra helicopters. They fitted them with the best that money could buy and promised more as soon as we arrived in Saudi. We, too, were given new equipment for the desert environment. Issuance of desert fatigues, hats, survival gear, and nerve agent antidotes was the last big step before deployment. I should say that was the "last big step" as far as the military side of things.

At home, many of us were scrambling to get our affairs in order. None of us imagined that we would be filling out our Wills at such a young age. That was definitely not the most exciting time in my life; more than anything, it served to show me what little I had to call mine. What I did have was sitting in an apartment that I did not know what to do with. Estimates, but only guesses, had us returning by Christmas. However, if that wasn't true...well, you can see the dilemma that I and other single soldiers had. There was also the matter of my car, my bills, and the rest of my finances. It was already apparent to me that I would probably be unable to receive and pay bills on time from Saudi Arabia. I could let my brother, Jeff, take care of everything, but adding to this problem was the fact that we still did not know exactly when we would leave. Also, there was that possibility that the Army would change its mind and not send us. If I had him come to Fort Campbell to get everything, he might wait forever, and I knew that he could not afford the long period away from work. This was a subject that disturbed me then and now. The military makes great efforts to assist families during such crises, but often allows the single soldier to fall through the cracks. This is a situation that still needs attention. Luckily for me, I had a best friend whose parents were more than willing to help and living in Memphis, only a few hours away.

As the days went on, final preparations were made. Our aircraft had to be flown to Jacksonville, Florida. One of the disadvantages of flying a Cobra is that we were constantly placed below the other attack helicopter, the newer Apache, in terms of priority. The Apaches would be airlifted to Saudi Arabia, and our Cobras would go by ship from the port at Jacksonville, Florida.

The flight to Jacksonville revealed some disturbing problems. Some of the environmental control units, or air conditioners, were not functioning. Although that is not a priority for two-hour flights in Kentucky, it is in the Saudi deserts. Unfortunately, we would not have an opportunity to repair them before they arrived there. The journey by sea would last twenty-one days, and the plan was for us to arrive a couple of days before.

Blowing in the Shamal Winds

NASA's Earth Observatory describes a fast-moving dust storm whipped across the Middle East: The plume of dust stretched hundreds of kilometers across Iraq, Saudi Arabia, Kuwait, Iran, and the Persian Gulf. The pinkish-tan dust softens and blurs the richer orange and tan color of the region's desert terrain and partially veils the olive-colored wetlands in southern Iraq. These large sand and dust storms are a significant natural hazard in the region and are often driven by fierce northwest winds called *shamal winds*. They blow in from the northwest with the passing of a storm with a strong cold front, which is the leading edge of a mass of cold air. The passage of cold fronts in the Northern Hemisphere often brings snow followed by strong west or northwest winds. In the Middle East, these winds scour the dust and sand off the surface and loft it into the air.

Now that you know more than you care about a Shamal, imagine flying a helicopter in combat through it!

A New Generation of Warfare and Tech

One must recall that the U.S. was still not over the failures of Vietnam (abroad and in how we treated our returning service members), and we were still confused by our emerging foreign policy in a post-USSR world. But it was the massive force arrayed against Saddam Hussein that evoked a renewed sense of power and purpose. Over 2,100 combat missions were flown in the first forty-eight hours of the war. Five-thousand tons of bombs a day rained on Baghdad—nearly double the amount dropped by the Allies in the 1945 bombing of Dresden, Germany.

And while the Air Force delivered relentless and pounding blows against the formidable Soviet-built Iraqi military, we sat bored to death, except for the terrifying nightly SCUD attacks.

The first Gulf War, commonly known as operations Desert Shield and Desert Storm, heralded in a new generation of warfare and technology for the United States. It was the first chance the Army had to seriously flex its muscles since Vietnam.

For our 101st Airborne Division, the war and its buildup were something it had never carried out in theater before. The division had to essentially move all of its hardware— helicopters, troops and ammunition— hundreds of miles at a time as we advanced toward Baghdad.

During the planning stages, there was a lot of uncertainty as to what type of military strength Iraq possessed. Hussein threatened the use of chemical weapons, which made for routine exercises involving soldiers rushing to put on protective suits and masks. Iraq's army ranked in the top five in the world in terms of size at the time. We were told to stay low, below radar and we might survive. That basically meant flying only a few feet off the ground.

On our first day of movement into Iraq, we flew escort for our ground troops deep into Iraqi territory. It was one of the proudest and emotional days for me in the Army. We were in the fight and those were my buddies on the ground. I would protect them at all costs.

Our division's mission was to advance on the Euphrates River valley south of Baghdad and there was talk of an air assault into the city, as the final step. With more than 60 UH-60 Black Hawks, 30 CH-47 Chinooks, along with Cobra and Apache gunships, the air assault on February 24, known as "G-Day," was recorded as the largest ever at the time. We flew through punishing winds and sand, killer temperatures and only feet off the deck. I am surprised that casualty numbers were not higher from the high-stress flight conditions.

Out of almost 700,000 deployed, only 148 U.S. troops were killed in action during Operation Desert Storm, and about 750 were wounded until the tens of thousands that would later suffer from Gulf War Syndrome and other illnesses that developed from exposure to massive toxic fires, nerve agent preventatives and other things.

Flying in the desert "balls to the wall", or as fast as the aircraft will fly, and low enough to require avoiding trucks all while reading a map, certainly hones your flight and navigation skills. It also keenly refined my risk assessment capabilities.

Flight Instructions for Leadership

It was a long journey to get to command that attack pilot's seat. I didn't think about making history in a gargantuan air assault. And little did I know then that my experience in Desert Storm would shape me in every way. It influenced the kind of man I am and greatly shaped the way I perform in the roles that I have had.

This experience and the period that preceded it, heightened my sensitivities toward injustice and compassion. This brief but intense moment in my life also brought me to understand the difference between a verbose leader and a warrior leader. One is real; one is not. One balances fierce commitment to mission with compassion for people, while the other barks orders and waxes about leadership by relaying stories of killing on the battlefield. I learned the difference between disciplined and reckless, selfish and selfless, good and great, and unifying and polarizing leadership. Every day, I try to emulate the best and learn from the worst. And every day, I work to apply the risk assessment tools that I am certain have led to the successes that I have enjoyed in business and other aspects of my life.

It's hard to believe that nearly thirty years later, I am still influenced by the lessons I learned half a world away. In business, I am an entrepreneur, so yes, I take risks, but I do it after serious assessments. I know so many people with "great ideas" that can't get them to reality. Forget the success part—I am talking about just getting the idea to market, period. I have been blessed throughout my life with strong male and female role models and I am sure that has helped me to understand commitment, not only to people but also, to causes. When I couple that gift with my experiences, particularly from Desert Storm, I find my discipline to accomplish the research and analysis needed before jumping into "the next million-dollar idea". And once approved in my mind, I remain committed to the effort through all the downs. Yes, there are ups, but in the beginning of an entrepreneurial effort, they are usually few and far between.

When you start flying, you learn in a disciplined and iterative process that is by the book. This is what helps you learn to fly and not kill yourself or anyone else. Later, as you have mastered the basics, then you begin pushing the envelope and bending, if not breaking, the rules to fit the environment. For example, the 1967 AH-1 Cobra model that I flew (67-15826 for all you history buffs—and yes, it is still active in a flying museum), was never intended to be equipped with the 1980s black boxes that mine had in the Gulf. When full of gas and armament, it exceeded its max takeoff weight by a lot! However, the environment that we were in meant there was no choice, so we busted the "rules" and flew overweight, which required bouncing the aircraft off the desert floor in order to get enough speed to make it fly. There is no way that someone just learning to fly a helicopter could accomplish this task without divine intervention. However, that does not stop countless entrepreneurs from dreaming big and jumping in without doing their due diligence. I often think these are the same people that open a box, throw away the instructions and start assembling. Please don't think I am being arrogant here; success in the cockpit and in business often requires a lot of luck. I am the guy that reads the instructions, so I am not simply reliant on that luck. As much as we all want, there is no fast way to getting rich (for the majority of us). However, with discipline and commitment, I think you will find that your successes outweigh your failures, which is what being a successful entrepreneur is all about.

I also believe that the Department of Defense should re-examine its entrepreneur track for transitioning service members leaving the military and returning to the civilian world. Here is the problem as I see it. There are plenty of examples of successful entrepreneurs that had no experience and little or no money and then made it big. However, that is not the norm and I would not wish this path on anyone that was not prepared. For me, I went into entrepreneurship with eyes wide open and a fallback in case I needed it. As I was leaving the Pentagon after serving both terms of the Clinton Administration, I had received a couple of solid offers that gave me encouragement and as I was assessing them, I received another offer to start consulting on my own. After great analysis, I chose that path, never to turn back. From my analysis, and this is a constant consideration, I knew that on my worst day, I could take a job that I might not like, but still be financially secure. That fallback provided me with the mental comfort needed to take the risk of striking out on my own. This is the consideration that I believe the DoD needs to ensure each person leaving the service should process.

Do you have a fallback? What is that fallback?

I also believe that before someone is approved for this track, they should be required to speak with an entrepreneur with a track record. I find that most are very engaging and willing to help.

What I am really trying to illustrate here is that we all should approach these situations and opportunities with the due diligence used in preparing our aircraft every day for battle. There is a process that you should follow and an assessment that is made. Sometimes you may choose to take the risk, but it will always be after the *analysis*.

CHAPTER 2

"Our deepest fear is not that we are inadequate. Our deepest fear is that we are powerful beyond measure."

—Marianne Williamson

I've been on this earth for over half a century, and it never ceases to boggle my mind how key childhood moments radically altered the trajectory of my life.

I was born in Texarkana, Texas, but there are few memories of my very young life there. What I do remember is living next door to my Mema and Papa (that's Southern for "grandmother" and "grandfather") and spending a lot of time in and around their house. In fact, the only memory I have of my house was sitting in the kitchen floor playing with Tupperware bowls and lids as my parents argued. That was about the time they separated and divorced. Memories of my biological father from when I was young are merely slivers of images and impressions.

Most of my recollections of growing up are centered around our home in the oil fields of Midland, Texas. As an example of the town's significance in the industry, the Permian Basin Petroleum Museum contains interactive exhibits detailing the history of local oil exploration and include Boom Town, a replica 1930s oil town with a land office and general store. And dating from 1939, the George W. Bush Childhood Home has been restored to its 1950s state when the 43rd U.S. President lived there.

We moved to Midland sometime in the early 70s, while I was still a young boy, the middle of three boys. My stepfather, the man I mostly knew as my father growing up, was a Fairfax vacuum salesman and had won a VW Beetle. I remember the family of four piling into this "car" for what would be one of the most uncomfortable trips of my life moving over 500 miles from Texarkana to Midland—even now, looking back and comparing it to the seating in combat helicopters, it was grueling!

Once in our new home city, we lived in a small rental house until we found our new home, a beautiful three-bedroom, 1 ¾-bath house with an awesome backyard filled with fruit trees. It was terraced, had a water fountain and benches. What more could a kid ask for? A super cool sandbox that would become home to countless deadly battles between solid green soldiers and large, hurling rocks from space. This was my escape and haven for my most cherished memories of play.

There were also great memories with family. Again, we were fortunate to have my grandparents, aunt and uncle move to Midland from Texarkana. That meant that as I grew up, there was a village to help raise me and my brothers. I remember weekends with the family, now five with my little brother, along with my Papa and Uncle Randy going cat fishing. There were small stocked ponds, where you could fish for a dollar a pound for each fish caught. That was our summer fun, with periodic trips to San Angelo, about 100 miles away, for weekend fishing trips. Mother made dinner at night and we would gather to watch TV after a hard day of play. When not fishing, the family would gather on the weekends for dinner at Mema's house, followed by rousing games of dominoes (the game of 42 mostly) and the occasional poker match. When I became old enough, I was allowed to join in, but until then, I watched intently and learned the strategies. In 42, "play to your partner and hope they cover your off." "Attack when your opponent shows weakness."

My mother had divorced when Jeff, my older brother, and I were young. She soon remarried and a few years later, gave birth to my little brother, Dana. I attended public school and did very well, not because I necessarily wanted to do well, but I knew at a young age that my high aspirations required a college education.

Coming of Political Age

At a young age, I got interested in politics, and not just through books but in-depth events swirling around me and conversation points from my mother, who I developed most of my values from. She must have known I would be the only kid watching Watergate, when she kept me home from school to witness history. The Watergate scandal changed American politics forever, leading many Americans to question their leaders and think more critically about the presidency. I was no exception. Except for the fact that I wanted to *be* President!

I went to elementary school carrying a Carter/Mondale sign for the 1980 election. Needless to say, Midland was not a liberal bastion, nor a moderate one. So, it was no real surprise that my Carter/Mondale sign ended up in shreds, along with my ego and arm that were quite bruised. Originally, I was not a Carter fan. We (my mother) liked Ted Kennedy. I grew up learning about Camelot and the Kennedys. I have no doubt that impacted me and my thinking, but me and my siblings were also encouraged to think for ourselves and today, my older brother and I could not be more different in our political views.

When we moved to West Texas and got involved in the oil business, a lot of guys had come to work carrying a dream and a bag. My mother insisted that we put them up in our house until they got settled. She worked every day, even if her efforts were as secretary for my dad's business. All my life, that is what everyone around me did—worked. I grew up learning that you tell the truth, play fair and take care of the weaker ones among us. I hate to see people take advantage of others.

Besides encouraging me to be knowledgeable about politics and take sides on world-defining issues, my mother was very open and loved to laugh. She was supportive. She loved to be involved with everything, from my shows in community theatre to school science projects. She loved to cook and fish (she would bait the hook but not take the fish off). For prom, she insisted that if we were going to drink, we do it at home and then made midnight breakfast for everyone. Mother didn't have a lot of desires or aspirations besides owning her own house, which is why when her final days would come while living in a rental house, my heart shattered to pieces.

The oil business went wildly up and down. We lost and regained, but Mother worked hard to splurge on occasional experiences. When we went to a restaurant every once in a while, it was always very high-end. When we flew that one time, I wore my little suit. I was going on an airplane! These experiences taught me cultural acumen and how to read menus in which the offerings of fish were out of this planet beyond the catfish I learned to catch.

Like most families in West Texas, our livelihood was the oil field. For context, in the 1940s, Texas had helped the US to overtake the Russian Empire as the top producer of petroleum. Some historians even define the beginning of the world's Oil Age as the beginning of this era in Texas. With vast exploration and development, this period had a transformative effect. At the turn of the century, the state was predominantly rural with no large cities. By the end of World War II, Texas was heavily industrialized, and its cities' populations had broken into the top 20 nationally.

To say the least, in the best of times, the oil business could produce overnight riches. In the worst of times, it could strip a family of *everything* in the blink of an eye.

Our first encounter with the worst of times occurred in the late 70s, only a few years into my family's new life away from vacuum cleaner sales. There was a tremor in the oil market and an earthquake in our family. In 1979, my stepfather walked out on us, leaving behind a trail of debt that he had accumulated and hidden over the previous months. It was a determined mother that found a better-paying job and did not skip a beat in taking care of the now family of four. Following her example, and at the age of 14, I joined my older brother who had already been working for several years. My first job, other than mowing neighborhood lawns, was as a bagger at Albertson's grocery store. My brother had worked his way up to a front-end manager and his girlfriend was a checker. Yes, it was work and sometimes not very fun, but all in all, these were some of the happiest months and years of my life. We were a family in rough times, getting through it together. That made the good moments even more special. With the work ethic deeply instilled, I never stopped and probably never will. In my teens, I worked at a movie theater, DJ'd at three different radio stations and even did a stint as a security guard...usually two of these jobs at once, all while keeping my grades up.

Though my brain wrapped around world events and the qualities of people who steered them or led people out of crises, I really fancied myself as an actor. I had been in community theatre for many years and enjoyed it—hey, I even thought I might be good. My mother did, too. She wanted me to go to New York to be an actor and not go to college. We were both unusual for Midland, Texas! Growing up, I realized I had a very unique voice and ability to manipulate it. I would sit for hours listening to

Marty Robbins on my mother's record player and shape my voice to mimic his. I did this with Neil Diamond, my mother's absolute favorite! Then one day, I saw a man on TV. He was doing hundreds of different voices of famous people. Rich Little made an impact on my life that stays with me even today. From that day forward, I became an impressionist—imitating the voices and mannerisms of what ultimately over the years became 136 different characters. Yes, the sheer boredom of sitting in Saudi Arabia during Christmas 1990 gave me time to count. I entertained family and friends with Presidents Reagan, Carter and Nixon, to cartoon characters of Kermit and Dudley Doright and songs from Carol Channing and Louis Armstrong, to Neil Diamond and Ethel Merman. It was a talent for fun, but it did pay for some of my college as I performed at the Improv and Funny Bone clubs around the South. It also helped take the minds of my fellow troops off their situation, as I performed stand-up shows across the desert in Saudi.

Looking back, I realize that I grew up in a city where the education system was excellent, the community theatre was recognized as being among the best on the map between New York and Los Angeles and the opportunities for unique work for a young man were plentiful. Now I know why my mother always told me, "You are a jack of all trades and a pretty damn good windmill worker." Still, I left community theatre to work fulltime at a movie theater while finishing high school and Jeff worked long hours to put himself through college and help the family. As I mentioned, these were rough times, but they and a strong mother are what also built our abilities to be independent. These are the stories of so many families, hardships that draw us all closer and closer. I don't recall any bickering over who would take out the garbage or clean the dishes. If something needed to be done, we did it. Nor do I ever remember a time that we considered giving up.

After a few years, the family had recovered and rebuilt. Mother married again, to a larger-than-life West Texas oilman—a man that I was convinced had to be the twin brother of country singer, Charlie Daniels.

The oil world had it pretty good, but when it turned south, it was horrible. This was the case through much of the early 80's. The 1980s oil glut was a serious surplus of crude oil caused by falling demand after the 1970s energy crisis. After 1980, reduced demand and increased production produced a glut on the world market. The result was a six-year decline in the price of oil, which reduced the price by half in 1986 alone.

The Savings and Loan (S&L) industry collapsed, people lost their houses and Midland became a shell of its former self once again. Near the end of my mother's life, we were one of only two houses on the block that people still lived in. I went to mow a neighboring yard and was stopped by an official from the government demanding I get off the property because it was government-owned. I suppose that could have had a chilling effect on my opinion of the "feds", but it didn't. It didn't because the woman that was dying inside our home taught me to respect those that serve, even an FDIC official that was just doing his job. My mother taught us a lot about respect and love for each other and our world. She passed a few weeks later, in no small part due to the stress that was unfairly put on her shoulders. I was not there to thank her for all that she had done for me, for all of us, but I think she knew.

As soon as I graduated from TCU, I left Texas with the intent of never returning. I had lost my hero and it was too painful to even think about being in the same space again.

A Speech, A Spark and a Hero Among My Sheros

Even after all these years, I still vividly recall the first time I heard John F. Kennedy speak. There I was, hopped up on sugar and banging away at pots and pans like a drummer at Woodstock. Then, out of either parental affection or simply the desire to escape an acoustic assault, my mother called me over to the television. It was the anniversary of Kennedy's assassination, and as an ode to his legacy, a local channel was playing his iconic "We choose to go to the moon" speech delivered at Rice University in front of an audience of 40,000. The speech had been intended to persuade the American people to support the Apollo program, the national effort to land a man on the Moon.

Up until that point, I had never in my young life experienced chills simply from hearing someone speak, but there they were suddenly quaking down my spine.

It was then my mother explained to me the power of words, how a great man speaking in the state I called "home" inspired millions to dream so big that not even the moon was beyond their reach. Looking up at the adoration in my mother's eyes as she delivered this wisdom, I realized we were feeling the same sense of enchantment.

At that moment, I wanted nothing more than to make people feel the way my mother felt about John F. Kennedy.

As I grew older, I became infatuated with studying important political speeches, viewing inspired oratory to be works of art equal to any painting. While other kids dreamed of being superheroes or star athletes, I practiced for the White House by reciting inauguration speeches to imaginary crowds numbering in the millions. In fact, I got so damn good at pretending to be the President that over the years, I added to my impersonation repertoire the voices of Richard Nixon and Jimmy Carter. Years later, I'd be using this talent to send the Speaker of the House, Jim Wright, into giggle fits, causing him to personally reach out and after a discussion about my life, he connected me with a position inside the Mondale campaign.

Historians view the 1984 election as a humiliating blowout, but to me, the Mondale/Ferraro campaign was a catalyst for tremendous personal and professional growth. I met lifelong friends that year who opened my mind and flooded my heart with an inextinguishable faith in humanity. To this day, we reminisce about trekking around the nation, building event sites in a frenzy, organizing into the wee hours of the morning, and then waking up a few hours later to ride along in a motorcade of station wagons. No amount of sleep deprivation could dull the exhilaration we felt from rolling up our sleeves and going to work each day in service of our ideals.

I remember being so convinced that Mondale would defy the odds, that he would prove the pundits wrong and hand Reagan a one-way ticket back to being a B-movie cowboy. Those rose-colored glasses were soon shattered, with the purest form of melancholy permeating across the team of bold idealists that had become my family. Even so, while he may have only won two states that night, Mondale forever earned my admiration: serving as an avatar of the leadership qualities I wanted to possess, someone who would speak the truth even when it failed to be convenient.

It is no secret that I consider Walter Mondale to be one of my heroes, next to my mother, perhaps the greatest in my life. "Why?" you might ask. I would point you to the movie, "Dave," which came out much later but spoke to a strength of this little-known vice president. People in power can behave sensibly and with good will in order to solve problems and unite the country.

Walter Mondale reflected in his life the truth that he stated in 1984. It was the truth that so many said cost him the election. He probably would not have won anyway, but we didn't know that at the time of the Democratic Convention and his statement, "Let's tell the truth…Mr. Reagan will raise taxes and so will I. He won't tell you; I just did." That moment of truth is all too rare in politics and perhaps absent in today's politics. But it was a truth that drew me to this American hero.

My hero, Walter Mondale, didn't know me from any other kid on the campaign or a crowd member at a rally, but he had an impact on my life. My mother had Ike, JFK, RFK and Ted. I had Ted and Walter Fritz Mondale. Maybe I was raised to look at the world through rose-colored glasses, but I know one thing to this very day: If you look through rose-colored glasses, there is not white, black or brown. Today, despite what I think might be the dawning days of the end of our democracy under the most hateful and unvisionary President of our lives, I still have those moments of true belief in the America, the American people and the American dream. Those days in 1984 may not have transformed my life, but they certainly shaped my life and have kept me focused and on track in even these darkest of times.

People are inherently good and that is the true definition of *liberal*. I still believe that good people, led by good people, will take back this country. I know, I have seen it. Call it the invigorating spirit of American exceptionalism. Call it blind faith in a pipe dream. Call it anything you damn well please, but I have seen devotion to America's fundamental promise radically transform lives, from West Texas to the inner cities of the Midwest. I have seen this higher calling cement unbreakable bonds between people from all walks of life, fostering a unifying sense of purpose capable of achieving feats long written off as impossible. This is the untamed belief and commitment that will not go quietly into the night.

Truth and Power: Sheros

Sharing the airspace with me in Desert Storm was the first woman pilot in U.S. history to fly combat missions. And she gave her life while flying in a combat zone. Major Marie T. Rossi died at age 32 on March 1, 1991, when the Chinook helicopter she was piloting crashed near her base in northern Saudi Arabia. The unit she commanded was among the very first units to cross into enemy territory, flying fuel and ammunition to support our advance deep into Iraqi territory. I salute Major Rossi for her courage and sacrifice.

You now know a little about my mother, who inspired so much of my principles and pathway. I think about her a lot these days. I see hints of her in a lot of the female leaders that I admire and advocate for. But when I consider where we stand in terms of women's piece of the pie in the military and in government, I cringe. I can't just say that our nation is merely behind—it's infantile, grossly underdeveloped. And why? The fact is that the whole system of governing has been formed by men for men since the founding of the Republic. Men are still 81 percent of Congress, 75 percent of state legislatures, 88 percent of governorships, and 100 percent of US presidents for the past 230 years. My husband and I have even discussed our belief that Americans are now more likely to elect a gay, male President than a female President and that just hurts. No one should want or accept excelling on the backs of others.

Untamed equality gets past these old pictures and paradigms.

Untamed equality does not know of language like "vagina voters" and "identity politics," which I heard so often during both of Hillary Clinton's Presidential runs. Untamed equality does not hold the belief that women legislators only tend to be clustered in the more progressive parties and only serve to promote "women's issues"—health, education, childcare, fighting discrimination and violence against women—more than male legislators do. I want all of these, as every functional, decent human should.

Untamed equality holds the truth that women should have equal power, or more, in every area of life, gaining that power in the same vein that men do. We can no longer move at a glacial pace. And that brings me to my next Shero, the woman that dared to step into the man's world and dared to be President. She may have been denied the shattering of the glass ceiling, but she put tens of millions of cracks in it.

CHAPTER 3

CHRISTIANITY AND COMEDIC RELIEF

"COMEDY IS AN ESCAPE, NOT FROM TRUTH BUT FROM DESPAIR;
A NARROW ESCAPE INTO FAITH."

—CHRISTOPHER FRY

I fell in love with languages in high school. I took French, German and Latin. I was drawn to the dialects and the culture. I was able to balance work, school and extracurricular activities and graduated at the top of my class. I even received an academic scholarship, but it wasn't nearly enough to cover the costs of college. With a little luck, a good job and my Pell Grant, I figured I could make it work.

My original plan was to go to Texas Tech; it was a short drive from Midland and it's where my brother and many of my friends went. But as my future was being plotted out in fine detail, I received a call from a friend who was going with his mother to visit Texas Christian University (TCU). It was a five-hour drive away, much more expensive and I knew no one going there except my friend. What the hell, and as my brother said, "Go if you can." I did and I never looked back.

During our visit to TCU, I explored the campus and went to the Air Force and the Army ROTC departments. As a future linguist, I assumed that the military was a perfect place to land. The Air Force ROTC was mostly in need of pilots and was limited on the number of slots it had available in their program, but the Army was excited to have me and even offered a scholarship. In the end, and as you have discovered from the previous chapters, unless you randomly opened to this page, I didn't become a linguist—I strapped on a flying machine!

Despite various other original plans, I would be attending one of the most expensive universities in Texas and a "Christian" one at that. I quickly discovered that despite scholarships, Pell Grants and a student loan, I was still short on funding for housing, food and party money. I immediately went to what I knew: finding a part-time job to pay the bills. I held several during my four-year education, from security guard for the wealthy Bass family, to NOAA weather radio, "the voice of the National Weather Service". Still, none of these gigs even remotely compared to my life as a stand-up comedian. My best friend in ROTC, who was also an around-the-town DJ, suggested that we take my knack for imitating voices on the road to make some easy cash at karaoke competitions.

oil market had tanked again, and this time, we were the ones to lose our home. My mother would spend her last days in a rental house, not the home she had dreamed of and saw taken away. The back-and-forth bus trips went on until the money ran out. I found myself in Midland at my mother's bedside and in my mind, I would not be returning to school, at least not now. Well, completely unsympathetic and deadpan, the lieutenant colonel of the Army ROTC program demanded that I return, or they would enlist me onto active duty immediately. As a scholarship student, I had an obligation to the Army. At that point, I hated this individual because I saw him as a horrible leader that had no empathy and I hated the Army because it was pulling me away from my family at its most critical moment. These emotions that I felt would eventually pass, but the memories remain and have helped me understand the impacts of the policy decisions that I have made in my public life.

Play Army

In my first year in the Army ROTC, we went into a field training exercise. *Play army.* A local National Guard unit flew us out in UH-1 "Huey" helicopters to where we would be doing maneuvers. Our pilots were a couple of crusty warrant officers that had flown in Vietnam. They decided to take us on the ride of our lives, so with doors open and *pop-pop-pop* of the rotor blades, we set off on what would be a life-changing experience for me. In that one short flight of maybe thirty or forty-five minutes, I saw the professionalism of these aviators as they constantly analyzed the risks of the flight while entertaining their passengers with a few scrapes of the treetops. Throughout the flight, they were laughing at us screaming like kids on a rollercoaster, but also talking amongst themselves in the calmest demeanor as they went about the work of the cockpit.

Upon that silly, fun and scary flight, I fell in love with the experience. Right then and there, I decided to become an Army helicopter pilot. To be perfectly honest, the *idea* of becoming a pilot was not something new and this wasn't a whimsical desire. I had been around and loved aircraft since I was a young teenager in Midland. I had even flown in Cessnas and joined the Civil Air Patrol. My other brother, Jeff, was also fascinated by aircraft and flying and eventually joined the Air Force as a weather observer and forecaster. My younger brother, Dana, became a commercial pilot and then eventually went to work with the FAA. The aviation industry has been a part of our lives for a very long time, so it was no surprise that I would set a course for the skies, albeit a little closer to earth than a jet.

Unfortunately, for my military career, and fortunately for humankind, when I was commissioned in 1987, it was during a downsizing of the military. This was at the end of the Cold War era right before the Berlin Wall came down, borders opened, and free elections ousted Communist regimes everywhere in Eastern Europe. America was "fatigued" by foreign relations and strived for a period of in-country prosperity. I was commissioned in the reserve forces, so my fellow classmates and I were shocked because we had planned on becoming fulltime Army officers. My degree was in political science and frankly, I was wondering what I would do for a job. Fortunately, as a scholarship cadet, I was guaranteed a slot to flight school so for at least a year, I would be okay.

In January 1988, I went to the Army Officer Basic Course, followed by helicopter flight school. At the time, we were made aware of a program that would offer active duty to those that finished at the top of their class. Well, I wasn't about to pass up on that offer. So, instead of enjoying the life of an officer at Fort Rucker, Alabama, I buckled down and hit the books, as well as extra sessions in the simulator.

The next time you see a helicopter propped up "perfectly" on a big boulder on the side of a cliff, consider the training that may have gone into that landing, at least in the military:

- Classroom instruction on the intricacies of rotary-winged aircraft. You learn basic flight physics, flight systems, emergency procedures, and you will learn how to draw and read flight maps.

- Quick advancement to Warrior Hall, where new pilots learn to fly helicopters in simulators with spider-like metal legs. Once you have enough simulator time under your belt, you'll step into the "real deal". For me, it was the UH-1. I was part of the first class dubbed "multi-track" where the goal was to get students more time in their advanced or specialized aircraft before going out to their units.

- Then on to becoming an expert in flying a specialized helicopter. Again, for me, it was the AH-1 Cobra attack helicopter. Much time is spent in this phase learning and executing advanced tactics. You're also taught how to fly with night vision goggles mounted on the front of the flight helmet. In my day, this meant offsetting the bulky weight with rolls of pennies taped to the back of the helmet.

After nearly a full year of flight school, I was set for graduation and yes, at the top of my class. As the Distinguished Honor Graduate, I received a lot of special recognition, a gift of silver wings and even got to give a speech. What I didn't get was an offer to enter active duty. Apparently, that program had been cancelled while I was busy learning to fly.

By now, you should know that for me, where there's a will, there's a way! In the final days before I left Fort Rucker, I started handwriting every member of Congress, all 435 House members and 100 senators, requesting to be placed on active duty. Most responded politely without much substance, but a few did reply that they would inquire with the Army. Strange that only a year and a half before, standing in Midland Memorial Hospital at my mother's bedside, I wanted nothing to do with the Army.

At this point, with completely cramped hands from all the handwriting (a lost art!), I left Fort Rucker for the "Land of Enchantment", otherwise New Mexico. I lived with my brother Jeff and his wife, Allison, and slept on their couch while trying to figure out my next move. During this time, I also did comedy shows in and around Albuquerque. I needed the money, and this was my original fallback!

One morning, I was out in my brother's backyard planting grass...no joke...and Allison came out of the house yelling, "Dick Gebhardt is on the phone!" At first, I thought, *no way*, but I rushed in and sure enough, it was Dick Gebhardt, the majority leader of the House of Representatives. He informed me to be prepared for a call from the Army and that they would be offering me an active duty position. And sure enough, they called within a matter of minutes. By this time, they had been hounded by at least a few of the 535 letter recipients!

"So, where do you want to go? What do you want to fly?" The sharp-shooting voice at the other end of the line was the warrant officer branch chief. The compromise was that I would give up my second lieutenant rank in the Reserves for a warrant officer rank, chief warrant II, on active duty. That was fine by me—after all, I was going to fly for the Army and get out of my family's hair.

So, I told the less than enthusiastic voice on the other end, "I graduated in Cobras and I would like to go where I will get the most flight time." Onto Fort Campbell, with the 101st Airborne Division "Screaming Eagles". If you come to know nothing else about the 101st or combat helicopters, just know that the 101st is recognized for its unmatched air assault capability and its ability to execute any combat or contingency mission anywhere in the world at a moment's notice – no offense, 82nd. Needless to say, I was thrilled beyond belief.

Persistence, I tell ya!

CHAPTER 4

ACTIVE DUTY, REACTIVE PERSPECTIVES

"POLITICS IS NOT A GAME. IT IS AN EARNEST BUSINESS."

—WINSTON CHURCHILL

In my lifetime of memories, since Richard Nixon, it seems that the Democratic Party has counted on the common sense of the American people to see it through. By contrast, the Republican Party has counted on the fear and anger of the American people to see it through.

It's worth noting that according to the Library of Congress (LOC), these parties were formed during the struggle over ratification of the federal Constitution of 1787. LOC explains: "Friction between them increased as attention shifted from the creation of a new federal government to the question of how powerful that federal government would be. The Federalists, led by Secretary of Treasury Alexander Hamilton, wanted a strong central government, while the Anti-Federalists, led by Secretary of State Thomas Jefferson, advocated states' rights instead of centralized power. Federalists coalesced around the commercial sector of the country while their opponents drew their strength from those favoring an agrarian society. The ensuing partisan battles led George Washington to warn of 'the baneful effects of the spirit of party' in his Farewell Address as President of United States.

You know I love a good speech! Well, on September 19, 1796, George Washington said, "Let me now take a more comprehensive view, and warn you in the most solemn manner against the baneful effects of the spirit of party generally."

I feel somber about both parties. Differences between the two parties are so stark that we seem to be at or near a point of no return in this time of the Trump Administration. Our citizens are paying the price of a government and at times, a military that do not serve them well. We have seen abdication of leadership at the highest level, the use of armed troops against peaceful citizens and concerted effort to divide this nation along racial lines.

As I mentioned before, my mother kept me home from school to watch the Watergate hearings, as it was a slice of history that she believed I should see. Yes, she was a Democrat, but being a "West Texas oil kid", I was surrounded by plenty of Republicans, including the rest of my family. To this day, I remember it, not to detail, but when I see any History Channel review or "Frost Nixon" movie, memories of those days sitting in front of a tube television in a small Texas house are as real as the days I saw democracy in action. It was a time when lying to Congress or refusing to testify was unheard of, no matter the party.

I decided to become a Democrat because I believed that this party would do things more like my family did. For example, when my father started a company and we gave housing to his salespeople who couldn't afford rent. Often, they slept on our floor in the living room until they could get on their feet. And again, when Ted Kennedy gave that moving and inspiring speech at the Democratic Convention in 1980. I wanted to be like those he was calling to action, like my parents, to help those that needed it most. These values still govern my life. I don't always get it right, but it isn't because I am lacking the passion and commitment.

When Ronald Reagan was President, I protested his war in Nicaragua within the events known as the "Iran Contra Affair" because I saw friends here that were separated and hurt by his actions. The United States provided money, material, and operational support to the Contras, various right-wing rebel groups in opposition to the socialist Sandinista Junta of National Reconstruction Government in Nicaragua. The purpose of the United States' Nicaragua policy during the early years of the Reagan administration is a matter of debate. When elected, Reagan promised to restore American power in the world, yet the complexities of that world forced a degree of pragmatism and caution on him, and he continued to work within the established international diplomatic framework. Reagan even refused to take direct action against Cuba. According to in-depth research by Brown University, when his first Secretary of State, Alexander Haig, told him at an NSC meeting that "you just give me the word and I'll turn that fucking island into a parking lot," Reagan showed reluctance to act. Reagan inherited a largely pacified region in South America, as nearly every country south of Costa Rica was secure under the thumb of dictators, of the kind lauded by President Richard Nixon and encouraged by Nixon's Secretary of State, Henry Kissinger.

Information emerged during the Bush Administration that the *contras* were major and systematic violators of the most basic standards of the laws of armed conflict, including the launching indiscriminate attacks on civilians, selectively murdering non-combatants including clergy, and mistreating prisoners.

Throughout this ordeal in the 80s, I realized that Americans are just some of the people on this earth, not all of the people. If we cannot respect others' rights to choose their leaders, then we are no better than those who force their beliefs on others. Thomas Jefferson said: "I hold it that a little rebellion now and then is a good thing, and as necessary in the political world as storms in the physical."

But I also recognize that Reagan was a popular and strong President that won a nation's love through his charismatic charm. How else can you replace double-digit inflation with double-digit unemployment and remain popular?

Walter Mondale, on the other hand, was honest and right when he said, "President Reagan will raise taxes and so will I. He won't tell you; I just did." A hero in my mind; a poor candidate, to say the least, in others'.

Despite wanting to be President myself, I chose to no longer focus on politics and instead, moved on to the Army. Besides, as directed by the Constitution, the criteria to be a presidential candidate is only to be a natural born citizen of the United States, a resident for 14 years, and 35 years of age or older. Not really challenging enough for me!

Fighting for Others' Freedom

Fortunately, I was fairly oblivious to the 1988 campaign and didn't regain political consciousness until it hit me square in the head. As I deployed with the 101st Airborne

Division to Saudi Arabia, in my mind, I knew why I was going. I had been summoned to free an invaded people (Kuwait). Iraq's refusal to withdraw from Kuwait after a seven-month occupation by a deadline mandated by the United Nations led to this military intervention by a United Nations-authorized coalition of forces led by the United States. That is what I was doing and how I justified this force to extricate Iraqi forces from Kuwait and protect our Saudi allies.

For each warrior, I think we must make our own peace for why we do what we do and despite all of the rhetoric about cheap oil, and that was my mission. But in the end, and certainly now looking back on those pre-Kuwait meetings between Hussein, Rumsfeld, and Cheney and the other neo-cons, I guess it was about cheap oil, too. Hussein may indeed, have been given the tacit green light; it wouldn't have been the first or last time such a thing happened. In any event, the reality was that a country was invaded, and innocents were killed; we could not stand for that outcome and that was all I needed to know.

The final deployment notice came on September 7th. We would deploy the following morning after a long afternoon and evening of acquiring our aircraft assignments and loading our baggage. By the time that I returned to my apartment, it was late. My best friend, Johnny, and I ate a pizza and drank our last beer for a long time. The nervousness had set in and neither of us could sleep, so we passed the time playing cards until we finally crashed on the floor of my empty apartment. That emptiness also filled my soul. What was about to happen to us?

It was September 8th when we all made that long walk across the tarmac to the awaiting jetliner. I will never forget that morning filled with tears from families saying goodbye to their loved ones, and as they cried, so did the skies. The rain fell in a very solemn way; not hard yet not a drizzle. The smell of earth was very strong at first until fumes of jet exhaust overwhelmed our nostrils as we approached the aircraft. We were boarding a Hawaiian Air L-1011 and I joked to another soldier that this was a "mistake" and "we were all going to Honolulu." It seemed to be the right time for humor, and she agreed. I could not get over the strange feeling of getting on a civilian aircraft while carrying a weapon. In reality, weapons were no problem; however, cameras were a problem. We had been instructed not to take cameras and that they would be confiscated. I think that there may have been a couple of soldiers that didn't bring cameras; for the rest of us, it was a matter of where to hide them.

Once on board, I immediately proceeded to the smoking section. This is where I would spend the first few hours of the flight, at least until the smoke got to me. In fact, the rear section of that airplane was worse than any bar that I had ever been in.

Our flight path took us through Gander, Newfoundland. On a somber note, this was the location of the crash that killed many of our fellow soldiers only a few years before. On a more uplifting note, most of the streets in Gander are named after famous aviators, like Amelia Earhart and Alcock and Brown, among others. Although we were not allowed off of the airplane, we could look out the door at the Cuban airliner that sat across from us. The temperature was freezing there, but before we knew it, we were off again.

Approximately 2,800 miles later, the next destination was Frankfurt, Germany. By the time we arrived there, our biological clocks were totally out of sync. It was daylight, but it was supposed to be late night.

Finally, we were allowed off of the airplane and herded like cattle into a metal building where we would stay for the next three hours, not an eventful stay in Germany. With everyone loaded back on the airplane, we began the final leg of our journey that would take us over Greece, Egypt, and finally, into Dhahran, a major administrative center for the Saudi oil industry.

As we entered Saudi airspace, the whipping up and crisscrossing of sand could be seen as far as our eyes could capture. Once again, my nerves sat in for what was to be a long stay.

As we were taxiing to our unloading site, I looked out the small window at a world that, in many ways, reminded me of my west Texas home. There were a few small shrubs but no trees to be seen. Suddenly, the aircraft jerked to a stop; this was it. We all moved quickly outside; at that point we still had no idea of what awaited us. Allied troops and aircraft crowded the airfield. This was somewhat of a relief to know we weren't alone.

The sun was setting, and the hot wind blew savagely, as if we were standing directly in the jet exhaust, and even the night did not bring any comfort to the temperature. By now, sweat poured from all of us and after what seemed to be a lifetime, we were loaded on board busses for the long journey to our new home.

Settling in for a Long, Hot Sleepover

At the risk of being rude and possibly causing an international embarrassment, the country of Saudi Arabia stank. Literally, it smelled worse than anything that I could imagine or describe. As we traveled down the road in a double decker bus, I was nearing the stage of physical illness. To begin with, I was sitting in the lower-level rear section, which was set aside for females only. The roof was 4-1/2-feet tall. We were each given a bottle of water, since the local water was non-potable. More liquid flowed though, as within a matter of minutes, soldiers urinated in their bottles since we didn't have a restroom on board. This in itself did not bother me; however, when that smell fused with the heat and the cramped quarters, it was nearly too much to handle.

I thought, *how can anything smell this bad?*

After about thirty minutes, the bus passed two large dump trucks that we had been following. It turns out that they were filled with rotting garbage. What a relief, thank God that the whole country did not smell like that!

The end of the journey placed us approximately forty miles from the nearest city. We had arrived at the unfinished King Fahd International Airport (KFIA). This was not a coincidence. The airport's basic infrastructure would support the operations and storage of all the Air Force A-10s, as well as the entire 101st aviation fleet of Blackhawks, Hueys, Cobras, Apaches and Scouts. It was a suitable place for equipment storage, but what about humans?

climate, the record high has been 128 degrees. Yeah, think about that!

"We Want Todd!"

Every blazing hot minute in that parking garage and in the air, fighting for democracy was worth it. Yes, I loved being a pilot, but flying as a combat pilot in helicopters was a completely different experience each time that I lifted off the ground. I've had friends killed in helicopters and I had rough landings, but no bad crashes. I loved the thrills and frankly, I loved pushing the envelope, like most aviators, I think.

We were told up front that we would last about eight minutes on the battlefield, because Saddam Hussein had all "the latest technology". We had old Vietnam-era aircraft that were struggling in the hot desert environment. We were told his radar system would pick us up at fifteen feet. A Cobra is twelve feet from the bottom of the skid to the top of the rotor. Do the math, that ain't much wiggle room. There were hairy moments. I almost ran into a truck while hauling ass back to re-arm. I flew through complete blackouts—actually, brownouts. When you land a helicopter in the desert, especially a powder sand desert, all of that sand goes right up in the air and suddenly you can't see the ground and the crew on the ground can't see you. We became skilled at landing helicopters in ways they were never intended to be landed. Find the spot and drive it into the ground, don't mess around and whatever you do, don't hover!

These physical risks are quite evident based on mere description. What is not easily digested is the high risk of being authentic.

It was Desert Shield before Desert Storm. When we first got to Saudi Arabia, it was very intense. We had to make it look like there were more of us than there actually were. Flights all along the border were the norm to make a show of a bigger presence. Once we actually started getting more troops on the ground, nothing was going to happen until we, the coalition forces, decided it would happen. So, there we were, waiting, waiting and waiting, bored to death.

What did I do?

I may have given up comedy shows, but I never stopped performing. My buddies had heard me do my best George Bush sending off the troops, so as the boredom hit, I started doing shows. It started in our small parking garage and then expanded to the units in and around the airfield. By Thanksgiving, I even had the 101st band playing backup for my musical impersonations. Louis Armstrong, Neil Diamond and all the Presidents rapping would entertain the troops across the desert, as units would send in helicopters to pick me up and take me out to their troops in the middle of the desert.

I will forever remember the day Bob Hope was to perform at the KFIA, our home. As is usual with trying to make something like this happen in a war zone, he was three hours late and there were thousands of us on the ground waiting. Imagine the scene, crammed together on a tarmac, sweating in the sun and hearing rumors that the scantily-clothed girls that always accompanied the USO star were not being allowed to leave the ship and enter Saudi territory—not an issue for me personally (more on that later), but for much the crowd, this was bad news.

Then the swell of chorus began. Soldiers started chanting, "We want Todd, we want Todd!" In that moment, I realized that this was what my mother meant when she encouraged me to follow my dreams. I realized then, that my passion for flying was different from my dream to perform. I didn't know what it all meant, but I knew they were different. What I did know at that moment was that troops were chanting my name and I was ready to stand up and say, "Hell yeah, get me on that stage!" Then came the voice, "Ladies and gentlemen, Mr. Bob Hope." Oh well, it was one hell of a Bob Hope show.

Deep down I knew and looking back from today and all that I have learned from others, I think I was using my talent to hide what otherwise might have been an obvious sign that I was...that I am...gay. Performing allowed me to act out, without coming out. It also provided the freedom for my fellow soldiers to be friends without having to ask me the question. But that didn't stop my company commander. Following this day of great fun in a place where little is had, my captain asked the question that sent thousands of soldiers, sailors, airmen and marines home, "Are you gay?"

Without missing a beat, I replied, "No". It was a lie, but I knew a "yes" would get me sent home and processed out of the military immediately. I wanted to be there, and I wanted to fight. Why deny me the opportunity to serve when I met the requirements? Why deny the country the money it spent to train a warrior to do this job? Questions that I still ask today when some want to exclude those who are able and willing to serve because they are transgender, have a tattoo, adhere to a certain religious practices, or are not a citizen. Stupid rules for modern times.

Truth and Power: Storm Stats

"Operation Desert Storm Was Not Won by Smart Weaponry Alone." This January 20, 2016, *Smithsonian* magazine headline brings me back. The piece is a fascinating romp through the war as it relates to the technology that was used. Operation Desert Storm has been deemed the "Computer War" and the "100-Hours War" purely due to the tech that this operation ushered through. My favorites: Holographic One-Tube light amplifying glasses that cost $25,000 a piece, and laser guidance systems on precision-guided munitions, like cruise missiles—18-foot-computer-guided flying bombs launched from warships. Pretty awesome at the time, but today, we watch these things all the time on CNN.

I want to take a moment here to share another statistic. The misguided view and mistreatment of gays who risked their lives for the United States to be successful in this operation.

As reported in *The Washington Post* by Jeff Stein in 1992, The Army's Criminal Investigation Division (CID) carried out hundreds of investigations of, among other crimes, homosexual activity in the ranks during Desert Shield and Desert Storm. Stein wrote: "The files, released to me under the Freedom of Information Act along with other felony records, show there were only four cases of

homosexual sodomy prosecuted during the August 1990-
July 1991 deployment of more than 195,000 Army troops.

"Sex among gays and lesbians didn't pose nearly the
disciplinary problem that old-fashioned harassment by
heterosexual men did. Army women filed at least 16 such
complaints during the Gulf War, on top of the many unfiled
incidents that have just now begun to surface in the press.
Those allegations range from repeated unwanted sexual
propositions to the uninvited fondling of breasts and
buttocks by enlisted men and even officers. The incidents
almost always involved coercion and threats. There were
also six court-martials for rape."

CHAPTER 5

EQUALITY INSIDE THE BUBBLE OF NATIONAL SECURITY

"THE DARKEST PLACES IN HELL ARE RESERVED FOR THOSE WHO MAINTAIN THEIR NEUTRALITY IN TIMES OF MORAL CRISIS."

—DANTE ALIGHIERI

Making it out of the "storm" in 1991, I was 26 years old and still thinking I would run for President of the United States someday. Coming home from war, the Army informed us that they were getting rid of Cobra helicopters and moving to the Apache, the new "advanced attack" brand. For those techy types who care to know the difference, the Apache boasted an improved nose-mounted sensor suite for target acquisition and night vision systems, an M230 chain gun and four hardpoints mounted on stub-wing pylons for carrying armament and stores, typically a mixture of AGM-114 Hellfire missiles and Hydra 70 rocket pods. The most pressing thing to know was that this new helicopter was built to improve combat survivability.

The choice before me was to learn to fly the Apache and stay on an additional eight years or stay with Cobras until they were phased out over the course of a few years. In that case, I would be going to Fort Bliss in El Paso, Texas, Fort Drum in New York (the coldest part of the state), or Korea, and continue the rotation.

The third option was to get out. I was an attack helicopter pilot that had been in combat, so I opted to move to the next phase of my life. I left Fort Campbell and drove to Little Rock, Arkansas, where I met with the Clinton for President team.

The campaign was excited to have a combat veteran on the team early on even before an official announcement. The plan was to bring me onto the staff following the announcement and by the end of the year. I went home to Midland, Texas, where I grew up and again, had planned to never return to, but I needed a job until I figured out my next major career move. I started working in the oil business, while anticipating that call from the Clinton campaign that never came. I had reached out a couple of times over the couple of months but heard nothing.

Finally, one evening, I called my campaign contact that ran the advance teams, and clearly under stress, he spat, "I'll call you when I'm ready!"

At this point, I had made up my mind that I wanted to be deep into the '92 campaign and to see where it would take me. I also was done once again with Midland. It was not where I would find my future. I called some old friends from the Mondale campaign and within a couple of hours, I was in contact with the Tsongas campaign, the other Democratic candidate for President. The next day, I was on the road to my first assignment, a rally in San Antonio, followed by weeks of nonstop events that took me from Texas to Michigan and Connecticut. Tsongas offered a somber analysis of the nation's economic plight in a book published by his campaign, *Economic Call to Arms*. He opposed a tax cut for the middle class but advocated one on capital gains to stimulate investment. In contrast to Bill Clinton's charisma and easeful nature, Tsongas offered a wry, self-deprecatory and occasionally moralistic message about responsibility. He began the primary campaign with a victory in New Hampshire and went on to win three other state primaries and the caucuses of four states before dropping out as Clinton won primaries in Illinois and Michigan. And poof! In one day, the Tsongas campaign ended (or suspended, as no one "ends" a campaign anymore), and I was invited to join the Clinton campaign. I was asked if I had a preference of working with the candidate, or his wife, Hillary. It had been a pretty grueling couple of months with Tsongas and frankly, I was a little tired, so I chose Hillary, thinking I might have an easy road of it. *Wrong!*

Hillary Rodham Clinton was breaking ground in many ways. She was not just the spouse of a candidate. She was a policy leader and had some very specific ideas about how certain things could be better in this country. I jumped from a busy campaign into a mind-blowing, nonstop, exhausting, exhilarating, motivating movement. For the next several months, I led the Arkansas First Lady through event after event, with larger and larger crowds. Although I was seeing her every few days, we had never had a conversation. Then, I was given the honor of 'staffing' their daughter, Chelsea, at the Democratic Convention in New York. This was an honor beyond belief. Maybe I make more of it than it was, but as a dad now, I think this was one of the toughest decisions they had to make, and I certainly hope I did them all proud.

After the convention, I was given another amazing assignment to staff Hillary in Hawaii. Jackpot! This would be the first time that Hillary (Mrs. Clinton) and I had a lengthy conversation. It was in a sandwich shop somewhere in Hawaii, between events. She asked me about my time in the Army and we discussed helicopter flying in the desert. It was not that long of a conversation and given that I was a reformed stand-up comic, I still don't know why I did and still do get tongue-tied around her.

I guess I didn't do anything too bad, since I found myself standing with Bill, Hillary and Chelsea on Election

Night in Little Rock. With the economy as his centerpiece, Clinton won a plurality in the popular vote and a majority of the electoral vote, breaking a streak of three straight Republican victories. He won states in every region of the country. Clinton swept the Northeast and the West Coast, marking the start of Democratic dominance in both regions in both presidential and statewide elections. Clinton also performed well in the eastern Midwest, the Mountain West, Appalachia, and parts of the South. As of 2020, to my knowledge, this is the last time a candidate won an election without winning the battleground state of Florida, as Clinton went on to carry Florida when he won reelection in 1996. This was also the last time that the states of Montana and Georgia voted Democratic in a presidential election, although demographic shifts in Georgia could make that subject to change in the near future.

I fairly rapidly went from helicopter pilot to high-flying politics.

This is the Real National Security

Throughout my life, I have gravitated to people who could have intellectual conversations, but that also have common-sense smarts. My mother, the first in her family to graduate high school said, "An education does not mean anything without common sense." I guess it worked for something.

After the election, me and my friends, including my best friend of thirty years now, Ron, took a vacation to Puerto Vallarta before returning to our homes. Back home in Midland, I needed to make some decisions about what came next. Soon, my friend, campaign colleague and Hillary look-alike, as many affectionately referred to, called. "Todd, what are you doing?" My response, "nothing" did not set well. "Get your butt to DC, we have a country to run!"

Well that was enough for me. I did not waste anytime packing and I was on the road to the nation's capital.

Of the thousands of people seeking positions in the administration, I was fortunate to have selected "her" when asked. I am not sure if I would have had the same opportunities if I had been part of the larger campaign structure. I was here and in the thick of it and on Inauguration Day 1993, I was standing in the office of the secretary of defense for a meet and greet, as the newly appointed White House liaison.

My role for the next several months was to fire the Bush people and hire the Clinton people. It was my first experience with the delicate balance of competing leaders bringing on their teams. The new secretary of defense, Les Aspin, had served for decades in the House of Representatives and as a result, had his own team of staff that he wanted to bring with him. This was a normal occurrence. But of course, I was part of the new President's team, and there were plenty of qualified professionals that had supported the campaign, thus the balancing act. Through what was often daily calls with Bruce Lindsey, director of presidential personnel, and negotiations with Aspin's team, I had placed dozens of senior appointees and created a new intern program to grow young Defense Democrats. I considered this to be one of my most significant accomplishments; the Party desperately needed new blood within our ranks, and this was a way to get it.

Finally, in June 1993, I moved into a new position that I had found for myself as the deputy assistant secretary of Army overseeing training, readiness and reserve issues.

The first thing you should know about having an office in the Pentagon is logistics. This immense structure is the largest office building in the world, claims four zip codes, and possesses a whopping 6 million square feet of floor space! The construction of the headquarters for the U.S. Department of Defense (once the U.S. War Department) has a storied history. The plans for the pentagonal design were based on the irregular shape of the proposed building site located east of Arlington National Cemetery. Plans for that location were scrapped, but the design and shape remained. In order to conserve precious steel at the start of WWII, the building is mainly constructed with reinforced concrete. Builders also placed a series of ramps throughout the building in lieu of steel elevators. The structure was limited to five stories in height and two subterranean floors, in another steel *(and skyline)* preserving effort.

We used to joke all the time how you could live in Crystal City, take the undergrown Metro to work at the Pentagon, and never go outside. I'm convinced there were people who did just that. You would see people working late nights and you would come in the next morning, and they would be doing the same task, as if they had faded into the woodwork at night only to reemerge the next morning. The reality though is that there are some extremely dedicated public servants working in the security of our nation, from the dauntless tasks of keeping the building clean and running, to implementing complex policies to support for our warfighters.

The first time I walked into that building on Inauguration Day 1993, I said hello to my small office and then the secretary of defense's office. I thought, *I'm here! I'm here!* For years, I felt like every day we were making a difference. There were times when I would have conflicts with senior military officials, going back and forth over issues, but it was always a capable, diverse team working together. We achieved a lot, particularly given that our administration was really the first to tackle the post-Cold War environment. President Bush had been focused almost entirely on Desert Storm and the economic issues occurring. He didn't have the opportunity to implement much, whereas Clinton implemented a great deal.

President Clinton was the first Baby Boomer-generation President. The White House describes his presidency as: "During the administration of William Jefferson Clinton, the U.S. enjoyed more peace and economic wellbeing than at any time in its history. He was the first Democratic president since Franklin D. Roosevelt to win a second term. He could point to the lowest unemployment rate in modern times, the lowest inflation in thirty years, the highest home ownership in the country's history, dropping crime rates in many places, and reduced welfare rolls. He proposed the first balanced budget in decades and achieved a budget surplus. As part of a plan to celebrate the millennium in 2000, Clinton called for a great national initiative to end racial discrimination."

An Untamed Approach to Equality in
Our Neighborhood

I got to see firsthand what it was like democratizing those former Soviet Republics. It was breathtaking to have the experiences and see the faces of people in Bulgaria and Romania, and how they were happy about our presence and outreach; it was remarkable. We partnered with these countries to teach and help them build military forces that would not lead countries but rather, report to duly elected civilian authority. Under the fist of Soviet rule, they had no knowledge or experience as to how a military is supposed to function in a democracy. This is what we embedded in their lives. It is the gift that the United States and our Western European allies gave them.

This is how I fundamentally feel about how we need to be approaching our own hemisphere. The problem we have in our own hemisphere is we only seem to care when they're creating a nuisance for us, or "sending us their rapists." Or when they're not treating our companies fairly, like United Fruit, we just go and invade. Unfortunately, history shows that we only have a passing attention span for our own hemisphere and it's a shame. We should adopt the model that we used in the early 90s to democratize the former Soviet Republics, which was highly successful, and we should take it to Central America.

If you want to decrease the illegal immigration flow into the United States, the answer is simple: Help them build their economies. Help them build their law enforcement structure, their legal, their military structure. Teach them to be democracies and stand with them. Don't go down there and fiddle around, like we've done many times, and lose interest and leave. I can't tell you how many times I have seen things like brand new Caterpillar equipment that we give to a country like El Salvador or Nicaragua in order to build roads, and they just leave it on the side of the road because it needs maintenance and we didn't provide any assistance on fixing, maintaining and operating this stuff. Where is the heart and soul in this assistance?

During my time in the Clinton Administration, I confirmed much of what I had learned in history and political science classes, as well as in business. I learned that successful international efforts require smart and committed oversight. You need a motivator, and that is true in business, too. For a country, why engage in Central America? It's for these other reasons. I don't care what the driver is as long as we get to the same end result. We need to make sure China does not get a foothold in Central America, which they have already done. Then you need a commitment, which means putting together a plan. In business, you have your eyes on profit, so you're going to stand up a division and execute the vision. In the federal government, you must move beyond studies and Congressional hearings and execute an approach that is built upon the successes we had in Eastern Europe. I believe it is beyond time to appoint an ambassador-at-large to Central America and engage the cross-agency tools necessary to make meaningful and lasting impacts in the region. Much like the work of DoD, Commerce, State, Agriculture, Justice and others working with Ambassador Strobe Talbott (Clinton's Ambassador-at-Large to the Newly Independent States of the former Soviet Union), we need to engage the full force of America's capabilities to secure the prosperity and the shores of our hemisphere—one coordinating individual with the responsibility and cross-agency empowerment to get the job done.

The White House adds in its description of Clinton as: "In the world, he successfully dispatched peace keeping forces to war-torn Bosnia and bombed Iraq when Saddam Hussein stopped United Nations inspections for evidence of nuclear, chemical, and biological weapons. He became a global proponent for an expanded NATO, more open international trade, and a worldwide campaign against drug trafficking. He drew huge crowds when he traveled through South America, Europe, Russia, Africa, and China, advocating U.S. style freedom."

Ask or Tell? Policies and Principals

The White House doesn't mention Don't Ask Don't Tell in Bill Clinton's profile of achievements. In 1994, when Don't Ask Don't Tell was instituted as a policy, I had to take a leadership position in implementing it. What exactly would I be implementing now as deputy assistant secretary for the Department of the Army?

In formal terms, the policy prohibited military personnel from discriminating against or harassing closeted homosexual or bisexual service members or applicants, while barring openly gay, lesbian, or bisexual persons from military service. This relaxation of legal restrictions on service by gays and lesbians in the armed forces was mandated by United States federal law signed on November 30, 1993. The policy prohibited people who "demonstrate a propensity or intent to engage in homosexual acts" from serving in the armed forces of the United States, because their presence "would create an unacceptable risk to the high standards of morale, good order and discipline, and unit cohesion that are the essence of military capability".

The act prohibited any homosexual or bisexual person from disclosing their sexual orientation or from speaking about any homosexual relationships, including marriages or other familial attributes, while serving in the United States armed forces. The act specified that service members who disclose that they are homosexual or engage in homosexual conduct should be separated (discharged) except when a service member's conduct was "for the purpose of avoiding or terminating military service" or when it "would not be in the best interest of the armed forces".

Don't Ask Don't Tell didn't just form in President Clinton's head as an acceptable policy for addressing the place of gays in the military. As context, the policy was introduced as a "compromise measure" by him on the promise to allow all citizens to serve in the military regardless of sexual orientation.

During the 1993 policy debate involving military personnel, politicians, scholars, and psychologists, which led up to the policy, the National Defense Research Institute prepared a study for the Office of the Secretary of Defense published as *Sexual Orientation and U.S. Military Personnel Policy: Options and Assessment*. It concluded that "circumstances could exist under which the ban on homosexuals could be lifted with little or no adverse consequences for recruitment and retention" if the policy were implemented with care, principally because many factors contribute to individual enlistment and re-enlistment decisions.

All rhetoric and theory aside, let me tell you what it really was from where I was sitting: an unmitigated disaster put in place by white, old men with no idea of where society was heading. However, it also represented an advance and the best deal that President Clinton could get at the time. We must remember that when it became obvious that Clinton would reverse the ban on gays in the military, Congress immediately began hearings in an effort to enshrine the ban permanently into law.

I can tell you that it was absolutely horrible for me to implement this policy. Everyone gathered in my office to watch the announcement on TV. It was a big deal for the military. I mean, just how many gays and transgender people I served with in Desert Storm is impossible to know. But I was there. I served and I am gay.

Eyes glued to Clinton's announcement, one of the colonels said something derogatory about "fags". I turned around to my executive officer, an army lieutenant colonel, and said with my finger in his chest, "You might want to let that colonel know who the hell I am!"

I walked out and slammed the door.

I had not publicly announced being gay, but I wanted to make it clear that anyone should be able to serve. The people in my department were often my biggest fans on the peripheral, but there was such a stigma attached to being gay—in a homophobe's mind, homosexuality is incompatible with all things military. Even as I stood there in a high-ranking leadership position for an office with 300 military and civilian team members; even as I had trained and served as a combat pilot, with specialized skills that helped us win a war; I was still gay and "incompatible".

New Frontier of Safety, Security and Inclusion

I detest the way the military has often been run like an old Southern city. But after all, most of our installations are down south. We recruit most of our enlisted folks from the Southeast and we target the most economically vulnerable and entice them with gifts of bonus cash, free education after service and a chance to "see the world", if not at least get the hell out of their hometown. The real problem lies in those families, often affluent, that do not have a stake in the game. They seemingly don't care if we send thousands of young men and women to Iraq to die because their families are not targeted for recruitment and probably have no ties to the military, thus no stake in the game. When everyone has a stake, they are less likely to support a war based on flimsy and questionable facts. They're less likely to kill thousands of their kids in an invasion of Iraq.

At the risk of really upsetting some, I do believe that at the time, Don't Ask Don't Tell was a steppingstone in the right direction of allowing everyone to serve their country but didn't go far enough. Transgender service should be allowed and celebrated. All positions, including all combat roles, should be open for capable women. The standards are there for every position. If you don't meet those standards, you don't get the position. It should be that simple, but it isn't.

In general, and perhaps sometimes shoving down the personal toll that Don't Ask Don't Tell took on me at times, there were three major initiatives that I went after aggressively during my time in the Clinton Pentagon with the goal of promoting different aspects of equality and fairness. Most importantly, these three initiatives began the practical basis for my call for untamed equality— what I consider to be the new frontier of safety, security and inclusion.

Better Opportunities for Single Soldiers (BOSS)

The philosophical foundation of the Army's BOSS program is based on the entitlement of single soldiers to surface issues and recommend policy changes that will enhance their overall quality of life, to participate in recreation and leisure activities of their choice, and to contribute to and participate in their local communities. This program provides an opportunity to assist in the development of single soldiers as *leaders* (or LEADERS, as I aspired to cultivate).

During my years in the Army, families were the main focus of attention and for the most part, our military was made up of a large percentage of families. However, as a single soldier, I and many others had no support mechanism in place as we were preparing our households for a long deployment. Our households may not have had spouses or children, but many had pets and all of us had belongings and bills that needed to be addressed by someone in our absence. So, when I had the opportunity to do something about it, I made the BOSS program one of my major focal points.

The mission of the BOSS program is to enhance the morale and welfare of single soldiers, increase retention and sustain combat readiness. BOSS sponsors a variety of activities before, during and after deployment to maintain the morale of single soldiers affected by increased operational tempo and deployment stress. The program has helped decrease suicides, sexual assaults and harassment and increase morale among single soldiers in the Army.

Creating a Fair, Realistic Readiness Reporting System Across the DoD

Clinton budget cuts to the Department of Defense (DoD) occurred in direct lockstep with the American public's demand for their Peace Dividend from the Cold War under Reagan. The problem was that this was in stark contrast to a Pentagon that had been enjoying increasingly larger budgets and was ill-prepared to execute on these reductions. Even otherwise cool and collected Colin Powell made a major scene about Clinton cuts to the DoD.

I learned here that National Guard units were underfunded because they were not needed in an imminent war deployment, yet they were graded for their readiness to fight in combat based on the same standard as a Special Forces unit that must be ready to go at a moment's notice. Anyone that has worked these issues inside the Pentagon or on the ground as a unit commander knows that if you are funded at one-third of your requirements, you will not be able to be ready for combat in a moment's notice and that in a post-Cold War environment with no major threats at the time, is okay. However, if I want the backup quarterback to be ready when I need him or her, then they need to get some time in practice, or I need not to expect them to be 100% ready to play at any moment.

A better approach is to say, in my military strategy, I will not need these National Guard units for ninety days after the start of major conflict—and by the way, that is exactly what we do. Then we fund these units based upon those needs. The disconnect occurred when it came to reporting readiness levels of these units, or their "fitness"/"ability" to deploy and fight. My approach was to have units report their readiness or "ability" based upon the requirements of the strategy. So, If I did not need you for ninety days and I funded you at that reduced level, then you should report your readiness level based on your ability to meet that ninety-day requirement, not a Day 1 requirement. I realize that this must seem drone and completely unimportant. However, in the world of the Pentagon and military funding, it is the centerpiece.

And this is where politics meets national security firsthand: Following the end of the Cold War with the biggest threat since Nazi Germany and before that, none since Britain, we had leaders, both uniform and civilian supported by the industrial complex that were fighting to keep funding levels at or near the same. That is why they pushed political narratives about the degradation of military readiness under the Clinton reductions. They could not see past the fact that the Cold War had ended, and Americans deserved their peace dividend. Pentagon leadership was spurred on by the industrial complex that was fighting to keep production lines open at all costs and budgets steadily increasing, even if the major foe on the planet had just disbanded. In one of my first meetings on the Clinton defense budget, I had generals demanding increased funding for military housing because despite the historically large budgets under Reagan, they had failed to replace the World War II wooden barracks and houses that still existed on many installations. So much for a peace dividend, we were facing a bailout of mismanagement.

And when it came to the narrative to support the increased spending argument, nothing was more effective than to talk about unit readiness. You see, if you do not intend to use a unit for ninety days and you fund it at that requirement level, but then ask it to report its readiness to "go to war" today, then guess what…it is going to report a lower level of readiness. Without explanation, you might look at that report and assume that this unit and others like it are underfunded. That was where politics and national security butted heads. If you reported a realistic level of readiness then the funding reductions might be justified: Unit 1 needs to deploy on Day 1, so it is funded and trained more and reports a readiness level of C-1, Unit 2 was needed in the Cold War on Day 1, but now, it is not needed until Day 90, so it is funded and trained to a level to be ready to go ninety days after the war begins. It should also be able to report a C-1 level of readiness, if it meets its level to be ready on Day 90. But that is not how the reporting system was used. It was a Cold War system, where virtually everyone needed to be ready on Day 1, being used in an environment where our strategy called for something different—not global thermonuclear war. So, as a result, this Unit 2 example, even if they were fully trained and funded to their required level to be ready to go on Day 90, they would still report C-3, which was viewed as a substandard level of readiness. What that meant inside the Pentagon was one thing, but when it was used by those seeking more Pentagon funding, it was a false narrative. And it was used effectively by those wishing to confuse the facts of the new world and make Americans worry about our security. In the end, some of the Clinton cuts were restored, but I was also successful in getting the DoD to change the way we spoke about and reported readiness levels.

Building a Cadre of Defense Democrats

I know that readiness levels do not seem at first glance to be an exercise in equality, but they are in my mind. When people or organizations are treated differently just because of who they are or the perceptions that others place upon them, I consider that an issue of equality. Another issue of equality is one that is prevalent across many organizations and many career fields, and that is the issue of age equality. When I arrived on the scene at the Pentagon in 1993, I was determined to bring as many of my fellow Hillary staffers as I could. Remember, I was the White House liaison, in charge of hiring the new Clinton team. Of course, the most senior-level positions were being handled by the President, his chief of staff and the secretary of defense, but the majority of the roles, and there were tens of dozens, were handled by my office in consultation with the secretary's chief of staff and the White House Personnel Office. Note that these are political roles, not career civil servants, so there is a level of loyalty to the administration that should be considered. The politician's job is to promote the administration's agenda across the Executive Branch. The civil servants are there to implement these policies, but also to provide the sanity check on bad policies, as well as provide the professional continuity that is essential to good government.

So, there we were with about forty of my colleagues from the campaign that had various levels of military and government experience, from college students to combat veterans, and the newly arriving secretary of defense team had a dozen or so of their own, including young staffers from Capitol Hill. It was the job of Larry Smith, counselor to the secretary, and I to come up with a program that we proudly named Defense Fellows, to expose these young future leaders to the Pentagon and the world of national security. After many days and sessions of deep deliberation, we created a concept to rotate these new appointees through various offices in order to gain exposure to the many functions of the department. From budget to legislative affairs, and from Army installations and environment to Navy public affairs, each new Defense Fellow would learn the intricacies of the machine that powers the most awesome force on the planet. We would grow the next generation of Defense Democrats.

That is something that I look back on fondly in the knowledge that we empowered dozens of young people that would otherwise have been overlooked and passed by, because as we all know every hiring manager wants experience, but you don't get experience, without the opportunity. People that we placed in this program have gone on to lead companies and work at senior levels in the UN. One is president of a Stanley Cup-winning hockey team and several advanced inside the national security community, including one who became a service secretary.

Looking past the dryness of how efforts toward military programs may sound, remember that the original mission was to serve those equally and totally who serve to protect democracy. That was my mission and it remains today; it extends to their families and friends, single and married, active and reserve, old and young...and lest we forget, gay, straight, transgender, male, female, African-American, Latino, Asian…and the list goes on, because it is only encompassed by "human".

Under two terms of the Clinton Administration, I was privileged to function as a primary point of contact with congressional committees, professional groups, media organizations, and other entities on these major issues and others. Needless to say, I heard and saw a lot—some of those sounds and sights being the antithesis of diversity and inclusion. Looking back from today, it seems almost like a time of repression and darkness, but it wasn't. From the small and big steps made in those years came the advances that so many of us enjoy today. Yes, the final change does seem to come quickly and often in a vengeance, but if we inspect history, we can see the chips in the various glass ceilings that eventually come crashing down.

CHAPTER 6

STRONGER DEFENSE FOR ALL

"IF YOUR ACTIONS INSPIRE OTHERS TO DREAM MORE, LEARN
MORE, DO MORE AND BECOME MORE, YOU ARE A LEADER."

—JOHN QUINCY ADAMS

When I left the Clinton Administration, I thought I would
be taking a few months up to a year off while the newly
elected "Gore Administration" got up to speed and before I
returned to a bigger and better role. Call it a silver lining in
a dark cloud or the overwatch of angels, sadly Al Gore did
not win, but that also meant that I was not in the Pentagon
office that was destroyed on 9/11, along with many of
my friends that were military, career civil servants
and contractors.

9/11 made an indelible mark on our nation and certainly
on me. The United States entered the days and weeks after
this horrific attack with the world's empathy—the world
had our back. However, it did not take too long before
we squandered that goodwill. The senseless invasion of
Iraq and the thousands of U.S. military and hundreds of

thousands of civilian deaths lingers as a sobering reminder that the good of a nation, even the United States can be reversed in a single decision. I was not part of the Pentagon during those years, but I watched as our military returned to a war footing and the casualties mounted. Although we had traumatic brain injuries and post-traumatic stress disorder (PTSD) in previous conflicts, we had never seen numbers like this. Because of advances in medicine and helmet design, service members that would have succumb to wounds in the past, survive today. The results created havoc in the DoD and the VA. Returning soldiers, sailors, airmen and marines were often sent home or back to units with hidden wounds that would eventually manifest in the form of physical and psychological problems and all too often, suicide. Eventually the numbers, almost 1 per hour, were so staggering that the military and the VA developed advanced programs to handle the wounded, ill and injured service members returning from Iraq and Afghanistan. It was during this period that I worked informally with my previous colleagues form the Pentagon on identifying markers for potential suicide, preventive actions and reintegration programs for those suffering from PTSD. Although this was and remains a passion, I still had to pay the bills.

In a formal capacity, I was earning my bona fides in the business world. Although I had held many jobs as a young man, I had not been in the commercial sector since I graduated college. As I described earlier, I started consulting on my own to a couple of companies that wanted to understand the inner workings of the Pentagon and the National Guard. I had been fortunate to have been taught about the complex defense programming and budget processes by my former executive officer, Colonel Marshall. Few appointees even today understand this process, but it is the most powerful tool you can have in implementing policy, for he or she who controls the money, has the power. This knowledge was important for companies, too, if they wanted to enter the drawn-out process of doing business with the military and I was able to explain it in terms that people could understand.

Consulting and working from home was fun for a while, but being an extravert, I needed to be around people. So, after a few months, I joined a small firm providing services to the government. It was owned by three retired National Guard officers that sort of viewed it as their source of money to support their golf outings. My joining this small firm immediately doubled their revenues. As I found my sea legs in the topsy-turvey world of government contracting, I quickly learned that all of that performing and radio dj'ing worked well in meeting and quickly connecting with people. Networking is essential in business and absolutely critical in government contracting.

Given my veteran status and time in the Pentagon, I was rapidly engaged on a number of business development fronts and within a couple of years, I had taken this virtually unknown firm from a few hundred thousand dollars in revenues to over $15 million a year. It came fast, but it was the result of a lot of hard work and at least one Christmas spent working in a basement on two different proposals. This was the start of many missed holidays and weekends, but I knew that if I was going to be successful, I needed to commit and it had to be my priority, just as I had done in every endeavor since entering the Army. I also knew that my clients had placed their faith in me, and I wasn't going to let them down; that meant a few 3:00 a.m. phone calls and several cross-country trips. I loved every minute of it, and I loved working with the professionals that came along to run some of the most important IT projects the military had. All of this also meant that my personal life and relationships took a back seat.

With my eye on the prize, I knew that my days in business were numbered, as I wanted to return to my love, politics. Although she was a rising star in the Senate, I knew in my heart that Hillary Clinton was destined for a Presidential run and with the defeat of John Kerry in 2004, I knew it would be 2008. The plan was to work hard, grow the company and sell my share, which became half by 2007. There is a whole other story to be told about operating and surviving in business. It is a world that frankly, I was not ready for. Perhaps my rose-colored glasses or what others might call naivete, I believed and still do that sharing the successes of a business with the employees that got you there was just normal; I think my mother would agree. Unfortunately, greed is a vice that is shared even among former "officers and gentlemen". I had to fight every year for employees to get their bonuses and as I left the company and sold my shares, I settled for far less than their value. That was mostly because my business partner knew I wanted to go and squeezed me for every penny he could. In the end, I may have left with less than I should, but I left with my dignity intact, a company of loyal employees that still have my loyalty and I was on my way to join the Hillary campaign.

My heart was in the fight and I was committed. Obviously, when Hillary dropped out of the 2008 race for the nomination, there was no love lost between the Barack Obama and Hillary Clinton campaigns. After eight long years of war and economic dereliction of duty under the Bush Administration, it was time for a strong Democrat President again and so many of us were convinced it was Hillary. But in the end, the majority of the party thought otherwise, so I quickly threw my support behind Obama and turned my newly refined fundraising talents for Hillary toward the general election and making Barack Obama our next President. Apparently, that was not enough. Despite numerous meetings with the new Defense Department's White House liaison, and a lot of pressure from well-positioned friends that knew my capabilities, nothing happened. Personally, it hurt.

Had I sold out my financial security for a dream that had ended? In the world of politics, the wave that carries you forward disappears and if you are not lucky enough to catch the next, you may be adrift. Washington, DC is filled with "formers" and I was not ready to be one of them. I was also not willing then nor now to be another insider that refuses to take the hard positions to make meaningful change, because it might rock the boat. These are the people destined to have their names in print and pictures on the walls of the agencies but remembered for nothing. As dire as my situation might have seemed to me at the time, it wasn't. My day would come again. Of course, there was a lesson in all of that; one that we teach our children, but sometimes forget ourselves and it comes in many colloquial forms: "sometimes you got to pick yourself up, dust yourself off and get back in the fight", "you don't always get what you want and that makes you a better person". There are many ways of saying it, but the lesson remains the same. In our struggles to reach our dreams, we will not always win, but failure comes only when we choose it.

I had to press on and once again, tap my entrepreneurial spirit. This time, I decided that I would keep it simple and consult on my own; no employees, no muss, no fuss. Hillary was the new secretary of state. Surely, her team would bring me in; after all, I had been a hard worker, was competent on the issues, I had given several of them jobs in the Pentagon and I had raised a lot of money for her. Surely there was a spot for me. Well, that didn't happen.

Was I mad? Yes. Did I feel rejected? Yes. Did I get over it? Hell yes. I knew this wasn't a Hillary decision and to be honest, I wasn't exactly beating down the door after the first rejections. I was off to make money. Before I knew it and despite my plans not to grow another business, I was back to consulting with several companies and then growing my own company with a handful of employees working on my issues of passion —wounded warriors, military families and equality across all of these areas.

Several years went by, and I would periodically try to reengage the administration for a chance to return to the world I loved.

One day, after a really bad day of work, my husband made a plea...one that he had made several times over the years knowing where my heart was. "Honey, why don't you reach out again to the Obama Administration and try to get in?"

I always monitored the ins and outs of the Pentagon, and I knew that my former colleague and a lady that I truly admire was serving as Secretary of the Air Force and had recently lost her undersecretary. So, I "made the call" (or email, in this case). And I was shocked that within a very short period, I received a response: The undersecretary role was not available, but she hastily sent a note to the White House liaison saying, "You need to get Todd back in the Pentagon."

After a few days, I had met with several people and was on a course to become the new assistant secretary of defense for manpower and reserve affairs in the Obama Administration. I stepped back to take it all in. There was groundswell of excitement and anticipation around this administration. If you go to the Records section of WhiteHouse.gov, you'll instantly notice that President Barack Obama signed, sealed and delivered the ultimate litany of social progress and equality initiatives, policies and laws. Approximately 200 to his credit. In essence, I was walking into a new era of equality, and I'm so glad I sent that email to another of my Sheros, Deborah Lee James.

Unlike with Bill and Hillary Clinton, who I met several times over the years that I served in the Pentagon, the Obamas I met only with dozens of others at various large-scale events and gatherings at the White House, never personally. Even so, my role would encompass a great deal of responsibilities that I hoped would do his agenda justice.

In the Clinton era, we had spent a great deal of time figuring out what was going to be the military's role in a post-Cold War world. There were a lot of debates about nation building and if we should be involved in that. What was going to be America's role? America's military role? In the Obama Administration, it was completely different. There, all of us would be tasked with focusing more on how to extricate ourselves from the longest war in our history. How would we help tens of thousands of the wounded and reintegrate these service members and their families back into society? What kind of programs can we develop to help these warriors achieve full and happy lives after they've been wounded and returned home?

The role of the Assistant Secretary of Defense (Manpower and Reserve Affairs) is to oversee all of the "people" programs and policies of the DoD. This included: military and civilian personnel issues, family support programs and the vast DoD school system. In basic terms, this meant I was dealing with issues like: the new DoD retirement system, Deferred Actions for Childhood Arrivals (DACA) and Military Accessions Vital to National Interest (MAVNI) programs, transgender policies for military and family members (particularly children), as well as the remnants of the removal of Don't Ask Don't Tell.

One discovers that airplanes and tanks don't have the thousands or millions of issues that people have and maybe that is why there are few that are really interested in the personnel roles inside the Pentagon. In fact, when interviewing for the position with the White House personnel office, I was asked, "Why personnel? Wouldn't you rather be in policy?" I realized that personnel supervision was not a coveted role, and rarely will win you any praise for getting things right, but it will certainly get you a lot of attention if you get it wrong.

Hiring manuals and job descriptions aside, when someone asks what I did in my role, I normally focus on the major issues that I tried to impact. All were centered on untamed equality, and here's a preview:

• Opening all positions for women (even in the 21st century, not all positions are rated on the requirements; some still were labeled "NO WOMEN").

• Allowing for open transgender service.

• Eliminating discrimination of transgender children of military members. The last thing our service members need to worry about is whether or not their family is being treated well.

- Creating transition programs that better position service members to leave military service with the skills and support they need to succeed when they return to the civilian world.

- Saving the Commissary program (low-cost groceries) that is a valuable benefit to military families in making a small military salary support the family.

- In general, creating an environment, policies and programs that supported a military that is more reflective of the society it serves.

"I Do, We Do"

One of the first initiatives that I worked on was spearheaded by Dr. Jill Biden, and it was brilliant and essential, and it came about as the military was grappling with the issue of spouse employment. We are living in a two-working parent world. And the fact is that we were increasing the number of breadwinners that were wounded, returning home and were going to struggle to get jobs. Spouses needed to seek employment, even in those previous single-breadwinner homes. The problem with this situation is that the service member gets deployed or transferred. Every three years, everyone and everything that accompanies that individual will need to pack up and move to a new location. Much of this effort was about creating stable opportunities with large, worldwide companies whose spouses could move to the locations and stay with the company—and create an understanding among the commercial sector. If you want to retain service members, employ their spouses. We were successful, thanks to Dr. Biden and a dedicated staff, with 100,000 spouses employed and major commitments from big and small employers.

I am committed to this still with my current company in employing spouses and activities that support telework so if they do get transferred somewhere, even overseas, that they can still do it virtually. Before the coronavirus pandemic, the Pentagon was one of those places that was less supportive of telework. Many leaders wanted face to face, eye to eye for every task as the military norm. That argument of so many jobs not being supported by telework has gone out the window. Now that we are many months into this new environment, there will be few companies or government agencies demanding everyone to be onsite. This will also help the military family, as more and more businesses evolve with virtual workforces.

The overall care for the military family will be an evolving trend and the future of the military. All too often, when we think of the All-Volunteer Force, we focus solely on the military service member. Certainly, without these soldiers, sailors, airmen and marines we would not have a force at all, but we can't forget the other critical elements of that "volunteer" force—the family. In the time of a conscript military, or compulsory enlistment of people in a national service, families were not a major consideration in the equation of drafting and retaining a force. Today, we may recruit a service member, but we retain a family.

Defense is Gender-Neutral

While I was in the Clinton Administration, I had played a significant role in the first effort to open combat positions for women. It started off by opening combat support positions, for example, artillery in which you're not on the front line, helicopter pilot positions. The right wing was already put off by the gay issue though. *We're attacking the old white men, threatening their power!* What happened under Obama was the natural progression of that process that had already started in the 90s, Navy Seal positions and Special Forces.

At this point, I hope that much of what I have written is beginning to come together; the experiences and things I learned along the way shape in every way my positions on policy. Employees should have a stake in the business and reap some of the rewards; people should be judged on their abilities, not on how they were created, where they are from, or the neighborhood where they live. All the military services have very difficult standards. If you meet the standard, *thank you! Come in!*

We need to get away from this notion that all service members must fit into this one mold. I do have a problem with the fact that we have not been able to graduate to the point where we look at an infantry soldier differently from a cyber soldier. If you are in computers and preventing the next hack from North Korea, I don't think you need to be carrying a forty-pound rucksack on your back as part of the requirement for your duty. All service members need to have a certain level of fitness, but beyond that, there is some differentiation that can occur. But in all cases, it is requirements-based, not gender, race, gender identity, sexual orientation, immigrant or any other irrelevant factor-based.

Working on the policy in favor of opening combat positions for women was a no-brainer for me. Working on the policy to permit transgender people to serve, however, was unbelievably fascinating. I was so passionate about this effort because of the role I had to play in the implementation of Don't Ask Don't Tell. I was not going to be part of something so polarizing and discriminatory like that again. Until the issue was laid before me in that role, if I had met a transgender person, I didn't know it. But that didn't matter.

Many believe that the Obama Administration was filled with people that believed in truly open service and that if you meet the requirements, you should be able to serve. That was just not so (and that is true in any administration), as not everyone is firmly in agreement with every position. On this particular issue, it went all the way to the secretary in terms of its obvious importance. But before he could see it, the policy went through the machinations of generals, admirals, deputy assistant secretaries, assistant secretaries, undersecretaries and service secretaries. This is the most critical stage because this is where a policy can be tweaked or even completely changed to be very effective or completely ineffective and worthless. So, when certain leaders wanted to require that transgender service members would be required to shower in bathing suits, I had to raise my concerns! Separate but equal is not an effective policy and frankly, if someone is checking out your "junk" in the shower, they are the one with the problem. Believe it or not, I faced a lot of opposition to this position, but in the end, that requirement, along with many other similar attempts, were thwarted.

I will repeat, my belief is that the military should reflect the society that it serves. That is applicable to every population, large or small. Gender identity and sex do not matter in meeting the standards to perform as a service member. Diversity is an organizational strength. This is how you make the most powerful military. If I remember correctly, a six-foot, blond-haired, blue-eyed military did not do so well!

And I want to say this loud and clear about untamed equality: Equality is not just about individuals. It is about organizations, groups of people, neighborhoods and families. We need to be equally inclusive of entire families. We cannot forget about children especially, our next generation.

As such, one of the first things I did when I entered the role of assistant secretary was insist that we have a Facebook account and interact with those that sent us messages. You have to be there for the people that you serve, and in whatever vein they engage with you.

There were several interactions with service members and families, as well as with the general public on a variety of issues that we were considering. Many were out of fear that I was leading an effort to destroy the military retirement system, with the implementation of one that would also offer retirement to those that did not serve a full military career. For as long as most of us can remember, you serve twenty years in the military and you receive a retirement for life. However, if you serve eighteen years, you get nothing. We were implementing the equivalent of a 401k for all service members, even if you only served one tour. Unfortunately, many believed that by expanding this benefit, we were somehow diluting or diminishing it for those who were planning to serve a full twenty years or more.

I have come to realize that there has been a deliberate stoking of fear in the American people over change… any change. Those, often from the right wing, promote the idea that if someone that was not getting something before, is now going to get some level of it, it must mean that it is coming from those that were originally getting it. In other words, the pie cannot grow and the only way for someone new to get a slice, is for everyone else to get smaller slices than before. This has been the case with rights for minorities and women; "giving them rights will somehow take away my full rights as a white man". It has been the case with LGBTQ rights; "letting two men get married demeans my marriage—even though I got married as part of a Fox reality TV show". It is a process of thought that promotes this fear that if we give a small retirement benefit to someone that only serves four years, then I will get less if I retire with twenty years of service. If we allow transgender service members to get medical procedures, then that will somehow take away my access to healthcare.

It is wrong, it is discriminatory, and it is used far too often to deny equality.

But I digress; let's return to the messages that I received through our Facebook page and what was one of, if not the most impactful that I received during my tenure. I received a message from a family in Germany, asking for help because their transgender daughter was being discriminated against in the Department of Defense school system (DoDEA). In their school, which had multiple buildings across campus, their daughter had to go out of her building and cross the campus to another building to use a faculty restroom. I am certain that this was not meant to be a nefarious decision by local authorities, rather one intended to ensure the privacy and perceived security of this young lady. However, decisions like this are often made in a vacuum or at the demand of some overly zealous individual with the same perceived "fear" as I previously described. What this message did for me was to immediately trigger my desire to reach out and level the playing field. This young girl, named Blue, already had enough on her plate and seemed to be doing well among her peers. She did not need adult interference where it was not needed. She also didn't need to be walking outside and across the campus, just to use the restroom. To me, this was a case of the "everyone just get along" policy of let's find Blue her own bathroom and then everyone will be happy, versus the "untamed equality" policy of hell no, that is not acceptable and she will be treated like every other little girl in that school.

In my mind, I knew what the solution was, but I also believe in truly hearing all sides and ensuring that I am not making a purely emotional decision. I assembled a small group to review the case and come up with solution options. In one week, I had a recommendation from a team of dedicated professionals, including career civil servants and military officers. By the next week, I had signed the new policy and Blue was able to participate in school, like any other kid. There were those within the school administration and DoDEA that didn't support this decision, some perhaps out of that perceived fear that somehow this would compromise the rights of other children (and it didn't). What it did was move the marker forward and say that equality is not just getting to be in school with other kids; it is being treated with the same level of respect and dignity. Also, it meant that her father was able to focus on his military job and not on how his daughter was being discriminated against.

Now, here is the kicker: Years later, my husband and I went to view a short film release at Human Rights Campaign headquarters. Filmmaker Brandon Kelley's short film, "The Real Thing", follows Allie (Sophie Giannamore), who has transitioned while her soldier father

(Michael Torpey) has been on an active tour of duty. The story depicts his acceptance and shows many tender moments. The film aired in honor of both Veterans Day and Trans Awareness Week. Well, little did I know that film was about Blue. She and her mother, Jess, were there as part of a panel after the film preview. It was a very emotional moment for all of us, as I let them know who I was during the Q&A session.

This is the enormous power of social impact. Impact is ever-lasting and perhaps it is no surprise that the mother of this transgender child sent me a personal note showcasing this impact further during the writing of this book:

It felt like a fight Blue and I were doing alone, just us against DODEA and the superintendent. It means so much to know we had all of you behind us, fighting for all kids like Blue!

It can feel so lonely and scary being the only out trans kid at a base. Being the family trying to protect our kids, and still serve. For months all we heard was "No," all we heard was "you're a child abuser for allowing your kid to be trans."

Thank you. I will never be able to tell you enough how much you saved my daughter and children like her. If you will allow me to tell you a short story. When Blue's story first made the news, I was terrified! I read the comments, and never have I ever felt lower in my life. Then I got an email from a family stationed in Japan. Their trans son was admitted to the hospital for his 3rd suicide attempt. He told his parents that if he was let out of the hospital, he would do it again until it worked. He had lost hope! They couldn't move anywhere he could be himself; his school didn't recognize him. His parents had just read the article in NBC where your policy was announced. His parents drove back to the hospital and convinced the hospital to let them see their son after visiting hours to show him the news article. They told him "you can go to school tomorrow and they HAVE to recognize you, as you". That boy started crying and that single thing was enough! Enough to give him hope that there is a life!

I know you did a million things as Assistant Secretary of Defense. But you saved that boy's life! You saved my daughter's life, and many more. You gave us hope when we had none. And I KNOW there is so much more hope left.

Affirmation like this makes advocacy worth it. I will always show up and speak up for what's right.

CHAPTER 7

Was it Ever a Secret?

"Hard times arouse an instinctive desire for authenticity."

—Coco Chanel

Authenticity is the new reality. I, for one, am glad to be raising a son in this new reality that I hope is never reversed. What can be more fulfilling than being who you are, true to your primal self and able to explore every facet of what that means for you personally, not your family of origin or an outdated idea of what family or self should be, rather truth...plain and simple. Although given the current environment, as I write this book, I am not so sure how permanent, permanent is.

You now know that when I got to the Pentagon under the Clinton Administration and became the deputy assistant secretary of the Army, I had to deal with the implementation of Don't Ask, Don't Tell. Within the walls of my workplace and externally in its consequences for our military and public image, it was a bizarre situation.

Simultaneously, I experienced internal conflict, of course. I will always remember President Bill Clinton standing there with all the generals. To his credit, he was fighting numerous battles on a lot of fronts. DADT was "better" than what we had before, which had been no protection at all. At least this way, other service members were not permitted to harass you about your sexual orientation, although it had to be kept secret, or not told.

However, people were being watched more. Truly, a soldier couldn't ask you, but they could certainly find out where you were going on the weekends. And they could send military police to gay bars. This policy would be in effect for nearly eighteen years, so go ahead and think about all the service members affected in that time period, and you feel the scale.

Because it was such a circus, representatives and senators got on a submarine in Norfolk and talked about this never working—"you can't have gays in close confined quarters with straights." Did they not realize this had been going on for years, decades, centuries? With all the stories swirling, it just heightened the attention on this issue to the point that the political right wanted to chase it.

Did I have a lot of internal conversations where I got pushback? Every step. By President Clinton's second term, it was obvious to most that I was gay. I wasn't advertising it or wearing it on my shoulder, but I wasn't in denial either. When I went into the Pentagon, I was 28, the youngest-ever senior appointee. I needed to grow a little, so by the second term, I was comfortable in my skin enough to pursue certain programs. Conflict really evolved around political factors—Clinton didn't come to DC with a large group of experienced Washington politicals available to him. Remember, the Democrats had been out of office for twelve years. A lot of people from the Carter era were brought in from the defense part of the house, along with key Republicans. There was a lot of gnashing of teeth and banging of heads. And in the Pentagon process, it often only takes one person at a senior level to stop an initiative. This is part of what happened in the 1990s with allowing service for openly gay members that ultimately resulted in DADT. It started to happen in 2016 with transgender service, but fortunately, we were able to override those reluctant voices and take another step toward a military more reflective of the society it serves.

There are always those that are reluctant to change, fear that the masses will arise and oust them from office, unable or unwilling to challenge those that are entrenched in the old ways, or just completely frozen in risk aversion and unable to make historic decisions without the counsel of the countless.

But just like these groups and stakeholders had to evolve, so did I.

Love is Love

Before meeting my husband, Junior, I had a long-term boyfriend. Even though my priority was work, he helped me evolve as a gay man working in Washington, DC and was the first to pull me out into the light of the gay community. Before this, I always wondered, *why do gay Pride parades feature the flaunting of men in nothing but tighty whiteys and women topless on motorcycles? Is that really helping our cause?* In this, I was naive, but I would learn. Like I said, I wasn't hiding, but I wasn't out proclaiming who I was and leading in the community. That would come later.

When I got married, all the family found out including the conservative distant relatives. All of my colleagues that didn't know, now knew. My whole philosophy had been, gay is what I am, not who I am. That changed after I got married. I didn't advertise it before—I didn't want to gain political favor for anything because I was gay. That was also a way to preserve the good relationships with people that might not approve. All that has changed since being married. I've become much more of an advocate for not only gay rights, but also, the Black Lives Matter movement. It is part of my firm belief in leveling the playing field of the human experience. The maturity of having a family and getting older, you begin to understand those people who used to dress in drag and ride motorcycles topless were not an embarrassment—they were making strides for the rest of us. Sometimes you have to grab the attention of people to make them change.

Junior and I had met online around my birthday in October of 2008. He was in DC on vacation and we met in a bar in the Dupont area. I asked him to come over for dinner the next night, and from there, we carried on a solid long-distance relationship, until we eventually decided that he would move to DC. He had been getting ready to go back to Brazil, where he was from, but I convinced him to stay.

At this point, I was fully engaged with the Obama-Biden campaign, while at the same time, considering a move to Miami, at least until I was hopefully back in an administration position.

Meantime, Junior's family flew into Miami to go shopping and then they were going on to Disney. I met up with him there while I was looking for property to buy. While we were there, I did an event for the Obama campaign. Al Gore came in to do a surrogate event, which

I put together. Well, this was an opportunity for Junior and his family to meet Al Gore if they were inclined. Within minutes, they were all on stage, this beaming, fun-loving Brazilian family who loved the United States. I really didn't think anything of it until the middle of the night, when it occurred to me that I put my new "boyfriend" and family members from Brazil on stage with Al Gore! Showy? Perhaps!

Needless to say, that night secured Junior's move to DC. Then we moved to Miami and I split my time between Miami and DC. We never felt settled in Miami, and I'm a political hack, as you know, so I just had to keep my roots in DC.

I proposed to Junior in 2011. Receiving an immediate resounding "yes" from the man I loved felt like I had won the love lottery. (And still does.) But what is fascinating is that "yes" seemed to set off the chain of events that would eventually lead to my return to the Pentagon and working for the most gay-friendly U.S. President to date.

A year or so into Obama's second term, a friend who had worked at the Democratic National Committee, informed me that he had gotten a call from the White House a couple of years earlier wanting to talk about me. They wanted to know about my background, experience and if I was gay. At this point he knew I was since after all, I was married in 2012, but at the time of the call, he still wasn't sure. The Defense Department operated in a fairly homophobic climate. Now, it's different. But in those years, it was still shaky.

It was a strange circumstance that because I was not active in my promotion of being gay, I may have missed out on an opportunity. Even my friends, when asked, were unsure whether they should say anything, being "outed" was still a thing and of course, no one wanted to hurt me, so they said nothing. It turns out that the administration wanted to vet and perhaps nominate a gay man for a senior Pentagon role. Well, I didn't get the position, but I learned a lot from hearing about what had occurred years before. Sometimes it is not enough to just take risks in business and policy; sometimes you need to step out and take risks in your personal life. Maybe not becoming an advocate earlier cost me this role, but as they say, with every door that closes, another opens. And think about it, they *wanted* a gay man. Do you think that the Trump Administration would have directly recruited a gay man?

Being married to the man I loved made me want to be more visible. Not just as symbolism of who the two of us were, but for the entire community worldwide. I wanted to march in a gay Pride parade untainted by my earlier negative judgment of being "out, loud and proud". We had every right to be proud and celebrate. So did every other gay person who had gotten married in the past year since the legalization of same-sex marriage. According to the Williams Institute at the UCLA School of Law, approximately 500,000 couples tied the knot since its legalization.

Junior and I thought about New York, Los Angeles, San Fran, and in the end, chose New York City, site of Stonewall. The staff were all too excited to have my husband and I march because of my record in the military and government—imperative entities but complex holdouts in the push for equality.

Scott Maucione, reporting for Federal News Network, wrote that the parade "wouldn't mean much for the federal government. Except this year among those marching was Todd Weiler, the Defense Department's assistant secretary for manpower and reserve affairs. Weiler marched openly as a gay man, husband and high-ranking civilian DoD employee. While DoD's civilian-side has not been as restrictive as the military in the past when it comes to gay employees, Weiler's march is a testament to the growing LGBT tolerance in federal and popular culture."

Unlike in years past, when I would have had more trepidation about being highlighted or exposed as a gay man in the Department of Defense, this was a new duty of mine and one that I proudly took on. Besides, the country was about to experience the first backward, brutal years of a homophobic U.S. President: Donald J. Trump.

CHAPTER 8

RUNNING AMERICA OFF THE RAILS

"THE DIFFERENCE BETWEEN A STRONG MAN AND A WEAK ONE
IS THAT THE FORMER DOES NOT GIVE UP AFTER A DEFEAT."

—*WOODROW WILSON*

After investing so much time, financial and emotional resources into two presidential campaigns for Hillary Clinton, not to mention years of waiting-room time, by 2016, we all thought, *God, please, not another Bush*! It never dawned on her most active supporters until a couple of weeks before that we could actually lose the general election to Donald Trump. This was the man who had just appeared before the American people in a video from 2005 bragging about assaulting women. This was the man, the candidate of the Republican Party for President that had mocked a disabled reporter in front of a rally crowd. This is a man that was regularly calling for physical attacks on hecklers in his crowds. And this the Republican candidate for President of the United States that said he "could stand in the middle of Fifth Avenue and shoot someone and I wouldn't lose any votes." Who in their right mind would voluntarily elect this type of man to the highest, most prestigious position in the land? I mean, we would never elect someone like this without major fraud in the election—maybe something like a foreign power interfering...

Well, it happened and as of this writing, we find ourselves in this spot again, with the 2020 general election looming. The difference is that we have an administration and party in the Republicans that is not only willing to accept outside interference, they are publicly seeking it.

He Drew Out the Hate and Made Us All Less Safe

For the last nearly four years with Donald Trump as our President, the United States has seen a rise in hate and hate-related incidents like nothing since the 60s. Trump has actively appeased white supremists and right-wing extreme groups, while promoting policies that hurt minorities, immigrants and mostly anyone that is not white and male. While doing this, he has also taken on an agenda that has made us all less safe. Either out of intention or stupidity, his administration has created an unsafe environment for our military, our children, our citizens and our world neighbors.

Our Troops Aren't Safe

The next time our military is deployed overseas and particularly to the Middle East, they will be facing a former ally that we left to die on the battlefield. That ally, the Kurds, may choose to forget and help us once again, but frankly, our history under Republican leaders in that region has been very sketchy, especially under this administration. Regional leaders have called Trump and his policies erratic and based on emotion. That is not leadership, much less LEADERSHIP. Under Reagan, Bush and Clinton, the military stood as a force for freedom and for the protection of human rights around the world. Our power was respected by friend and foe alike. The erosion of that stature began under George W with the invasion of Iraq. It improved and began to rebuild in terms of worldwide respect under Obama, but then was decimated under Trump.

I am not talking about the equipment superiority or the commitment and professionalism of the forces. I am talking about the world view of our forces. True military leaders never want to use the awesome force of our military units. The hope is to deter through respect and yes, sometimes fear of that power. What eats away at this is the retreat of forces from engagements with no reason and leaving allies in the lurch. The fear may remain, but the respect that is needed to give pause to foes and reassure allies is eroded. This must change and the only way that will occur is through a purge of this administration and public accountability for their actions.

Veterans Aren't Safe

I have worked to create transition programs that better position service members to leave military service with the skills and support they need to succeed when they return to the civilian world. We still have the strongest military in the world, so why are there tens of thousands of veterans homeless? After putting their lives on the line for our country, veterans must navigate the lack of affordable housing and economic hardship that everyone faces, but often, they are doing it while trying to recover from the memories of a seemingly never-ending war. When it comes to outreach, testing and support during this pandemic, I don't exactly think the Trump administration has prioritized any efforts for the veteran community.

Unfortunately, our veterans are without untamed advocacy—you know, the kind that refuses to take no for an answer. Yes, there are organizations that have been around for decades, some for over a century, that are dedicated to veteran issues. However, for many of these organizations and the veterans they serve, there is simply no attention at the national level, and I am unsure of their ability to truly mobilize and demand action. I believe that our veterans should be joining the Black Lives Matter movement. Why? Because it is the right thing to do, but also, because there is much that is shared between these groups of Americans. Fighting for a cause, suffering at the hands of callous leaders and unattached bureaucracies, needing a massive movement to attain untamed equality. Our veterans have much to offer and much to learn from BLM.

Immigrants Aren't Safe

In addition to veterans, immigrants, the foundation of our nation are also not safe. Immigration concerns have only intensified over the course of decades, because there is no comprehensive immigration reform, because there is no immigration strategy. Security, economic and humanitarian vulnerabilities are making America remarkably unsafe.

Established in 2012, the Deferred Action for Childhood Arrivals program — or DACA — defers deportation proceedings for two years for qualified individuals who were brought to the United States illegally when they were children. The program also gives those who are approved work authorization, and the approvals can be renewed. The millions of people who had once been protected under DACA are not safe.

During the height of the pandemic, nearly 203,000 DACA recipients were on the front lines of the coronavirus fight as workers in healthcare, education and food services. The Trump Administration stalled work permits for those whose protections expired or were set to expire soon. For some, their fate is still unclear. Why would anyone reject people whose capabilities could help to manage this crisis? This is just another example of the race-hating policies and a peek into a nonsensical response to our public health caving under a lack of resources. The DACA program is indicative of the unfair, unjust and uncaring immigration system we have today. For the millions that remain in the shadows, they are not safe. These are Americans. It's so sad to see people stand up and say, "Send them back to where they came from! They're taking our jobs!" Think about it. Undocumented immigrants and DACA recipients do not wear these labels on their bodies or clothing. So, when people make these attacks, I must ask them, are you really angry about undocumented immigrants, or DACA recipients that were brought here as children and had no say? Could it possibly be that you have an issue with people of color? Undocumented isn't a term solely owned by Latinos. If you met me, you would have no idea if I was a citizen or an immigrant, legal or illegal. Is this complaint really about focusing the frustrations of some that have seen their jobs outsourced or eliminated onto a population that has become villainized? We have a term for that, and it has reared its ugly head way too high in the last few years.

How did we get here? How did the immigration system get so broken?

I believe that the system is broken because there is no strategy, therefore, there is no logical process for a program to support that strategy, and thus, we have a broken system.

A fair strategy for immigration policy must encompass care and equality. You must have a sense of caring for people, not just your own, in order to have the empathy to support an immigration policy that does not just favor the economic needs of the U.S. You must possess an eye toward equality in that you can truly look at all humans equally and see the value in all. With these values as a base, then you can find the tools, the strengths, that immigrants bring to the fabric, the safety and the security of our nation as well as the world. Immigration of desperation will continue and should be a strong piece of our policy, but it should not just be about opening our doors to those that are fleeing. It should be about strengthening their nations to provide for their people and become better stewards in the community of nations. It also means recognizing that the world's leaders have major responsibilities in addressing the problems we create that wreak havoc on these countries, like climate change.

The migration issue along our southern border is an unsafe situation in the best of times, and a disastrous one now. Children die while living in cages separated from their families. Our neighbors are coming here because they are scared for their lives and looking for a better place. For the people fleeing El Salvador, we are sending them back to a death sentence at the hands of gangs that are often led by criminals that did their time and learned the trade here in the U.S. And when you think about those from the gay community in Central America or South America, that almost always signifies torture. How can a country with Lady Liberty as our beacon to the world knowingly reject someone fleeing certain fate?

This is an approach that I believe can work. The two actions below, I referred to in Chapter 5. Here they are in more specific detail:

1. Assign and deploy a special envoy to establish an agreement on creating processing communities on both sides of the U.S.-Mexico border. As part of this negotiation and commitment from the U.S., we should deploy FEMA and military resources to

establish "temporary" communities with housing and resources (water and food). These communities would serve as temporary respites for migrants and asylum seekers. While on the Mexico side, people would be processed and given background checks to identify violent criminals that could pose a threat. With the cooperation of Mexican authorities, we would detain and return these individuals to law enforcement in their countries of origin. For those posing no threat, they would then be moved, with their family, children included, to the U.S. side for continued processing and either temporary work permits or the beginnings of the asylum process. By centrally locating these facilities, we can focus asylum judges to these locations and increase throughput. We can also focus the resources of nonprofit and NGO organizations to these border communities to assist. By providing humane and expedited treatment, we will focus the flow of undocumented immigrants to these locations. This is not an amnesty program, but it is a documentation and indoctrination program. By providing even a temporary opportunity that is legal, with the promise of a repeat return, we could tap the labor resources that we need, while providing the support that our southern neighbors need. However, this step does not work, without the second.

2. The United States must invest in our own hemisphere. We cannot continue the failed practices of half-assed engagement that led to despot dictators, gang violence and rampant intolerance. We need a multi-billion-dollar campaign to encourage business, support democracies, build civil police and volunteer militaries and tap the amazing resource that is the people of these great countries. As I previously mentioned in this book, our program would in many ways mirror the programs implemented across the former Soviet republics and Eastern-bloc countries. Under this Special Envoy, all necessary agencies would participate (DoD, State, Justice, Agriculture, Commerce, Labor, DHS, etc.). The investment must be real, and it must be long-term. The results will be economic gains for all, a stable hemisphere and a border that is not flooded with people fleeing the certainty of corruption and death at the hands of gangs and dictators.

You will hear every reason imaginable that these two actions are not feasible. But they are. It's not a genius's phenomenal plan, but it is doable and sustainable. We did it for those that look like us in Europe, and we can do it for our own hemisphere.

Allies Aren't Safe and Foes Aren't Safe

That line, Foes Aren't Safe, seems strange, but let's peel
it back. One of the things that makes our nation and our
military abroad safe is the certainty of our resolve and
action. We strive to ensure that our allies know that we
will be there when they need us. Our foes know that we
will hold them accountable for their actions. Part of our
strength and the respect that we have garnered even from
our enemies is based on our predictability. That is not in
comparison to the element of surprise. It is, however, in
relation to a predictable and measured response. We are
not going to nuke Iran over an incident in the Gulf. It is
when this certainty is removed that safety and security
is threatened.

Predictability and surety of action was critical to
keeping the world from nuclear destruction. However,
under the unpredictable, emotionally based policies of
Trump, our allies wonder if our resolve continues. The
administration's public statements and actions toward
our NATO allies call that into question. Our enemies are
emboldened by the unsurety of our actions. Will we back
down again if Russia invades another country? Will we
hold them accountable if they are linked to the murder
of our troops? Will we allow the murder of our reporters
for the sake of lining personal pockets? The steady
chipping away at the resolve and surety of action has

consequences that have yet to be seen and will have long-term implications.

Safety and security are not arbitrary catchphrases. We cannot possibly feel safe under rash decisions. Or extreme actions in areas that are not top priority. Or inaction in areas that most certainly are top priority—like a once-in-a-lifetime pandemic.

We Aren't Safe

I was struggling with whether or not to address the ongoing pandemic in this book, but then I realized that this truly is one of the most consequential events of our lifetime. So, as I sit and consider the myriad of elements of humankind (success, failure, egoism, heroism, narcissism, and altruism and many more), I am drawn to write about what I see from the once rose-colored glasses that I wear. And this applies to pandemics or other gargantuan crises that call for the utmost leadership, care and coordination.

We have shown our ability to come together and unite against a common threat. We sacrificed as a people during the years of World War II and the Great Depression; yet today, we can't make it through the basic protocol of wearing a mask for even a few weeks to prevent the spread of a virus that has no cure. Some Americans have expressed blind rage when asked to wear a face mask in public. Psychologists deem this bizarre response to a worldwide pandemic as resistance to inconvenience and response to mixed messages. I call it abdication of leadership and a public adrift. The "mixed messages" reasoning clearly comes from our current White House occupant. Though Americans are dying at alarming rates from coronavirus, President Trump was not seen wearing a mask until July 12, 2020. At the same time, he was declaring that the virus, which he also has referred to as a hoax, would magically disappear. According to the database website, Factbase, Trump used the expression "Chinese virus" more than twenty times between March 16 and March 30, 2020. A photographer actually captured the script of a speech wherein Trump had crossed out the word "Corona" and replaced it with "Chinese". Leaders don't run their mouths amok like this, spewing falsities and xenophobia, and not be held accountable.

Today, we see the litany of video posts of Trump followers refusing to wear masks, shouting down those left in the precarious position of trying to enforce company policies in order to protect their customers. These scenarios that are played out over and over again on the Internet and news broadcasts, did not have to occur. LEADERS lead. My mother taught me to take the harder right, than the easier wrong, and we have been fortunate to see some state and local leaders following that rule and enforcing the medical advice of masks and social distancing. But they are not supported by the administration and especially the President, so the result is chaos and a death toll that continues to rise. Grocers, restaurant hosts, gas station attendants, people just trying to live their lives in a safe and healthy manner, are being forced to confront a mob of often belligerent crowds hell-bent on exercising their "rights" to infect anyone and everyone they come in contact with. Let there be no doubt, this is the result of leader abdication at the highest level and as a result, we are now the biggest spreader of the virus in the world. We are not safe in this environment and this must change.

As I woke from another slumber wrapped in the warmth of my white privilege, I wiped my eyes and as they cleared, I began to read of another night of protests, looting and pain. In one day, Black Lives Matter protests peaked with half a million people turning out in nearly 550 places across the United States. That was a single day in more than a month of protests.

My country was burning and no matter how much I wanted to help, I began to understand that no amount of empathy from the outside will change the situation inside of our communities of color. I began to understand that to really change this situation, we have to be inside of it. Maybe that was what my mother was teaching me throughout her far too short life. I would like to think that she had cracked this nut, like many others of her generation that found peace and harmony in diverse communities.

So, let's take this simple premise and build upon it. The pain cannot be fully understood (if ever) and the solutions of hope cannot be developed and implemented without being inside the situation. If this is true, then the first step is to actually be inside of these communities and not just when a police officer murders their citizens. We have to sit down and listen to the mothers, fathers, children and elders. We must hear what they need, what they are crying out for, in order to truly begin the process of understanding.

What has come to the forefront of my mind, as I realize what I am witnessing, is that the burning and yelling is a sign of desperation of people that are at their wit's end. Our communities of color...OUR COMMUNITIES, OUR PEOPLE...are hurting. They are hurting from the lack of quality education for their children, quality healthcare for their families and neighbors, security for their community and hope. Hope has been replaced with despair and the complete disregard for their plight from our white privileged communities is the straw that has broken the back of civility. So, we can complain about the destruction, but deep down we must understand that those of us that enjoy privilege have contributed to this destruction. We have become deaf to our own and now they are lashing out, even at those of us that have empathy and want to better understand. And throwing the military into this mix is not only unhelpful; it is dangerous to everyone and to our democracy. We must, at all costs, keep our military separated and revered by its citizenry, not seen as a force on one side or the other. Our communities are not battlespaces, and this is not an occupation.

Untamed equality does not allow for the prioritization of property over people. It does not allow our nation to move forward any further without addressing the inequalities that continue to exist in our communities of color. Untamed equality forces the agenda forward even at a time of a global pandemic. It demands that change occur; no more waiting.

The empathy that I feel for this community did not just start, but it hasn't been with me all my life either. To know the true suffering is to know the need for healing. We all must find it within us to reach out to our communities of color and bring us all close into the hug of humanity. Then we can all begin to understand each other's fears, needs, hopes and dreams.

I mentioned the use of military forces in responding to civilian protests. It is important to note that for many, there is little distinction in their understanding of a military

service member or a military-clad law enforcement officer
when they are facing off with peaceful protestors. This is
a distinction that we must address from the national level.
Our citizens must never have reason to fear our military,
period. And placing our troops into compromising
situations, like Lafayette Park, is a dereliction of duty by
the commander-in-chief. This does not make anyone safer.

And our safety has been compromised in other areas
as well.

Policies of Isolation

We pulled out of the Paris Accord.

In December 2015, President Barack
Obama envisioned how we should leave today's children
a world that is safer, when he announced that the United
States, along with other nations, had committed to
the Paris Climate Agreement, an ambitious global action
plan to fight climate change. Note that 197 countries—
every country on earth, with the last signatory being
war-torn Syria, adopted the Paris Agreement. And then...
President Trump announced that the United States would
drop out to join only Turkey, Russia and Iran in not
following commitments from all major emitting countries

to cut their climate-altering pollution and to strengthen those commitments over time.

We made a separatist speech at the UN Assembly.

On September 24, 2019, President Trump made these remarks to the 74th Session of the United Nations General Assembly, clearly pushing the "America First" ideology and nationalism in direct contrast to the ideals of the UN.

I have the immense privilege of addressing you today as the elected leader of a nation that prizes liberty, independence, and self-government above all. The United States, after having spent over two and a half trillion dollars since my election to completely rebuild our great military, is also, by far, the world's most powerful nation. Hopefully, it will never have to use this power.

Americans know that in a world where others seek conquest and domination, our nation must be strong in wealth, in might, and in spirit. That is why the United States vigorously defends the traditions and customs that have made us who we are.

Like my beloved country, each nation represented in this hall has a cherished history, culture, and heritage that is worth defending and celebrating, and which gives us our singular potential and strength.

The free world must embrace its national foundations. It must not attempt to erase them or replace them.

Looking around and all over this large, magnificent planet, the truth is plain to see: If you want freedom, take pride in your country. If you want democracy, hold on to your sovereignty. And if you want peace, love your nation. Wise leaders always put the good of their own people and their own country first.

The future does not belong to globalists. The future belongs to patriots. The future belongs to sovereign and independent nations who protect their citizens, respect their neighbors, and honor the differences that make each country special and unique.

It is why we in the United States have embarked on an exciting program of national renewal. In everything we do, we are focused on empowering the dreams and aspirations of our citizens.

Talking about "national renewal" to our international body of allies, stakeholders and even policy "enemies" at an annual summit for the United Nations was unwise, to say the least. Trump's speech and his continued promotion of this nationalistic agenda mirrors the pages of history that chronicle few memorable leaders, and those were mostly despots. Looking back almost four years into these policies, we see what it has done for us. We are more isolated than ever, we are alone and the biggest contributor to the spread of a global pandemic, we are failing our allies and emboldening our traditional enemies. Not exactly a position of safety and security.

We pulled funding from the World Health Organization (WHO) during a pandemic.

In April 2020, Trump announced he would suspend funding to the global public health agency, pending an investigation into what he called its "role in severely mismanaging and covering up the spread of the coronavirus."

This rash move threw several key health programs—funded in part by US contributions—into disarray, including the agency's emergency fund to help at-risk countries across the world fight the coronavirus pandemic.

"This is the most counterproductive move in the middle of a world health crisis," said Megan Doherty, a senior director of policy and advocacy at Mercy Corps and a former White House National Security Council director for North Africa during the Obama administration, for *Foreign Policy*. "In places with poor health infrastructure that don't have an existing strong presence, this is creating a gap that we can't fill."

Trump's decision threatened the fate of other public health and vaccination programs around the world, beyond the current pandemic. "What it will do is rupture global vaccine programs, polio eradication, Ebola response, and a thousand other global health tasks that the U.S. relies on WHO to deliver," said Jeremy Konyndyk, a former senior USAID official now with the Center for Global Development.

As of this writing, globally, we have more than 18 million confirmed cases of COVID-19, 672,000 deaths within a six-month span, no cure, no treatment program.

The safety and security of our country and its people has always had challenges. We have weathered man-made disasters in the form of wars, economic fallouts, discriminatory policies and practices. We have faced massive storms from mother nature and have responded in each occurrence with resolve and determination to rebuild stronger than ever. But it is a rarity and at this point in our republic, historic, that we would be facing a safety and security challenge from the very top of our governmental structure. It is man-made, because we put it there through our actions or lack thereof. It is a reflection of our darkest side as a people and it feeds off of the fear and anger that darkness perpetuates. It is not of our better angels and it is not in the spirit of what has made this nation the greatest on the face of the earth. The administration of Donald J. Trump is the personification of an important reminder to us all: Lack of vigilance on the part of every American to protect this fragile experiment can lead to its demise.

CHAPTER 9

BRINGING IT ALL HOME

"THE SECRET OF CHANGE IS TO FOCUS ALL OF YOUR ENERGY,
NOT ON FIGHTING THE OLD, BUT BUILDING ON THE NEW."

—SOCRATES

In our world today, which despite our problems is still
quite amazing, we remain unable to fulfill the promise
and need of equality. We cannot accept the status quo,
a country where our fellow Americans are subject to
pain, torture and death because of their color. Yet, under
our current ideas of equality, that is exactly what has
happened. We have paid lip service to all but the smallest
of changes. We have allowed the amount of change to
be measured against the standard of do no harm to white
privilege. The system is broken, and it needs to be fixed.

Just as in times past, we are seeing the pushback—the
fight of untamed equality. We see it in the Black Lives
Matter movement; we see it in the mothers linking arms in
Portland and the athletes kneeling at the anthem. We are
beginning to hear the voices calling for...no, demanding

action. This is what our country is really about in its purest form. We must achieve equality at the most fundamental levels of safety and security.

And unlike in the past, there must be some accountability for action. It cannot be enough to say that mistakes were made. We must learn from the past and destine to never repeat it.

At this point, I hope that it has become clear that within equality, its afforded safety and security is not just protection from white supremists or bad cops. It is about the safety and security of the whole, as we are not safe and secure, if any of us are threatened. This is an issue of national importance, national healing and national security.

Promoting a world of true equality may be different for each of us in its application. It may be recognizing that baking a wedding cake for a gay couple hurts no one and actually lifts up everyone. It may be ensuring that the officers that are facing off with protestors are led by someone from that community and will talk first and often before ever considering the use of force. It must be about ensuring that our military is a mirror of the society it serves. Most folks don't sit around thinking about national security, what the nation's threats are, or what needs to change. But being the passionate advocate for untamed equality, I do!

I've already made the case that it all starts with leadership—strike that, I meant LEADERSHIP (we're near the end, but remember the intro). Decades ago (ouch, that's hard to say), as a young aviator, I saw defense as defending democracy and the physical borders of our country. Today, however, I strongly consider equality as what we should ultimately defend—this also encompasses democracy and borders.

Making significant and meaningful change within the federal bureaucracy requires time, talent and a lot of perseverance. No place is this more evident than inside the five-sided structure known as the Pentagon. Changing this department that consumes well over half of the federal discretionary spending is like stopping an aircraft carrier on a dime. It is a department whose very structure has evolved into a behemoth that sprawls beyond the imagination of most and whose bureaucratic processes are designed to resist change. This is not always a bad thing. After all, we wouldn't want radical and overnight changes made to our nuclear arsenal. But change must occur and, in some forms, like personnel, may be warranted at a speedier pace.

Before any deep discussion of change can occur, a lesson or reminder is needed for the hundreds of millions of Americans that live outside the beltway. Unless civics classes have changed, I recall no education course that covered the true workings of the federal bureaucracy. Therein may lie much of the problem—perception is not reality when it comes to the DC machine. For many across the country, DC is synonymous with inaction or bad action. As I have explained to my family in Texas on many occasions, you may not always like the product that comes out of DC, but you can never complain about the productivity. Here, work is life and life is work.

I count myself as a well-educated man, yet before my arrival in Washington I never understood the role of a political appointee. I never knew that today there are approximately 4,000 political appointees in the federal government attempting to drive the administration's agenda...well, usually. Adding to the mix are approximately 2.1 million federal civil servants; these are career personnel that are mostly responsible with ensuring that the various federal programs and departments function on a daily basis. We know what the military is, but many will not know that the military has representatives in many different agencies other than the defense department. Between these three groups of uniformed and civilian personnel, Americans across the nation receive services from the federal government, from social security checks, small business grants and loans, safe passage into some of the most beautiful parks in the world, to yes, the safety and security of the most powerful military on earth.

The changes that we often seek and that I am promoting in this book are often started by the political appointees within the various federal agencies, as they follow the directions of a presidential administration. Real and lasting changes occur when the bureaucracy, or career civil servants support these changes. Without their support, changes fade with the term of the administration. Within the defense department, change is further complicated by the presence of uniformed personnel. This now trifecta of political and career civilians, along with military leaders, creates a fascinating dynamic that adds to the struggle for change. Again, within the national security arm of our government, this is not always a bad thing; however, it can also stifle badly needed changes, particularly in the areas of personnel—remember Don't Ask, Don't Tell. This means the job of political leaders inside the Pentagon is more…intense. But when it comes to the safety and security of our people, it is well worth it.

As I think about bringing all of this life experience and exposure to good and bad leaders and policies, I see real opportunity for substantive change within my world of expertise.

A New Century of Personnel Issues Facing the DoD

We may be twenty years into the new century, but because of endless wars, the Department of Defense personnel system has struggled to keep up with new generations of Americans.

According to the U.S. Census Bureau, Millennials (ages 18-34 in 2015) now outnumber Baby Boomers (ages 51-69 in 2015). Numerous studies about this generation indicate a group of people that are patriotic, but unlike their predecessors, not to symbols of patriotism, rather the democratic values of equality and opportunity. Many commonly quoted studies point to a narcissistic, over-confident, entitled population with little empathy. However, these studies focused across the breadth of the generation. Pew Research conducted a series of studies and one in particular focused on the later stages of the Millennial Generation.

As reported in the *New York Times*, "What Pew found was not an entitled generation but a complex and introspective one—with a far higher proportion of nonwhites than its predecessors as well as a greater number of people raised by a single parent. Its members also have weathered many large public traumas: the terrorist attacks of Sept. 11, costly (and unresolved) wars, the Great Recession." This study found a transformed and quite different later millennial from one of the 1980s. This population is generally skeptical of institutions, both political and religious, and they are far less interested in monetary wealth, preferring a work-life balance. We are all aware that these later millennials and the follow-on Generation Z are extremely tech savvy, but they also have far less concern over the "big brother" aspect of the digital world. This crop of young people has a high level of entrepreneurial spirit and a "do-gooder streak", with 54% of those surveyed from Generation Z indicating that they have a desire to make positive impacts on the world.

How do we apply what we know about this generation and help shape the future defense structure for our nation? Taken together, the signs that we see for the generation of current and upcoming military recruits and officers is not one of self-promotion and narcissism, but of empathy, open-mindedness and open hearts to people, animals and the planet. These insights should go a long way in helping us shape our messaging and targeting for the future military.

Building and Retaining the Next Great Force

Raise your hand if you think that college is affordable. Sorry, I can't see you! Whether community college becomes free for some or all and university debt is waived or greatly reduced, the impacts on military recruiting will be profound. History shows that when an issue has this much support, change will follow—untamed equality.

With fast retiring baby boomers and a historic 32.9% decline in GDP, or $1 trillion being wiped out of the economy as a result of coronavirus, we had best pay attention. When we look at the primary factors in the recruitment of young adults into our military, the message is clear: It is time to reassess. Our commerce will need vast numbers of workers from labor to engineers as our nation rebuilds; the military will be competing with these demands, but perhaps we should take a different approach and consider opportunities of cooperation. It is in everyone's interest to ensure a strong military, while building a strong economy. In today's environment the idea of service first has taken root and is now expanding. Where we can support America with service following education, then delivering these educated, trained and committed individuals to the commercial marketplace, everyone can win.

Our Millennials have a large sense of service and empathy to their communities. These are people that want to help others and serve a greater purpose; although the sacrifice that they are willing to endure may look different than that of previous generations.

So, what are we to do within the DoD to reach this population? One is to reshape our message to this group of young Americans. We should communicate, without hesitation, a call to service and appeal to this emotional and empathetic audience. We should highlight the opportunities that exist to serve the nation, serve your people and have a meaningful experience in the process. Instead of sharing posters of tanks and fighter jets, our new generation of service may be drawn to the work we do to help the world in fighting plagues like Ebola or rebuilding after earthquakes and tsunamis. The logistics capabilities of our military not only make us the most lethal force on the planet, which we do not need to over-advertise to our potential recruits, these capabilities also make us the best in disaster recovery and nation building force available.

Many years ago, we targeted the opportunities of travel and unique experiences. Information today shows that these are things that attract this new generation. When we look at other factors that these age groups are looking for in work, they list work life balance, opportunity to achieve success and enjoying a full life. The time has come for us to reassess on a broad scale, from recruiting to retention, family programs to retirement.

For possible tactics, let's talk social and gaming in the recruitment process. Pokémon GO didn't go away. *The Verge* reports that it experienced a massive viral launch in 2016, followed by a sharp decline the next year and has since rebounded to record revenue numbers again. It was intended to get young people off the couch and walking around the community and because of its individual player attraction, is a fun game even during a pandemic. With a $30 Pokéstop, companies have attracted thousands of players to come to their businesses, according to *Tech Crunch*. Yet, in my research, this multi-billion-dollar phenomenon has not one military recruiting station as a Pokéstop. Our recruiting stations remain in strip malls and although we have improved in the virtual recruiting environment, there is so much more to do.

If we want to attract and retain this generation and the next into uniformed service, then we need to get away from military golf courses and into gaming areas, community forums and more active opportunities on social and IRL (hmm...the old guy even knows that one). Social media is woven into our daily lives, whether it's three minutes or three hours of use. So, why aren't we using it not only for recruitment of the new crop of service members and their families, but also for retaining them?

Once we have successfully recruited a military force, we must retain it. In the pentagon, we have a phrase, you recruit a service member, but retain a family. Therefore, we need to change the way we think about retention. It should not solely be based upon the needs of generals, senior officers and senior enlisted. We need to listen to the needs of our newest recruits and families. They are not asking for more post or base exchanges (military retail stores); they are asking for education opportunities, stable and transferable jobs for their spouses, good schools for their kids, childcare and eldercare. All the things that we see large corporations offering to their employees, are the benefits that our military families are asking of the pentagon. Soon, I believe, they will be demanding. Remember, untamed equality is not just about individuals. Groups of people that are ignored for long periods will force a change for equality. And although offering priority golf slots to senior officers and retirees may not seem like a big deal, it is representative of bigger equality issues. In the end, we will listen and make the necessary changes, or we will see our recruiting numbers fall and service members leaving. The time has come for a complete reevaluation of benefit offerings and the needs of military families.

Although I promote the importance of smart business practices in the defense department, I also recognize that in some cases, priority must be given to military family needs. An important example is the commissary system. These are our grocery stores on most installations that offer discounted, high-quality products found in most mid- to high-end retail grocers. Does running a military grocery operation make good business sense? In a purely commercial environment, probably not, given that there are grocery stores in the communities just outside the gates of our installations. However, in most surveys of military families, they rank commissaries at the top of their list of desired benefits. Even still, this is a benefit that is under attack from the purely business elements from within the Pentagon, as well as certain politicians that are supported by retail grocery lobbies. This is an important example of how the pendulum swing for smart business practices has gone too far. Policy offices, like mine that are in charge of family benefits, are being subjugated to chief management offices that are charged with looking only at the dollars and cents of programs. There certainly needs to be business process and fiscal review of all programs, but wholesale elimination should not be based on pure business decisions. The Pentagon and the military families that support our security are not a business. There must be a balance.

When it comes time to leave the service, we need to work harder to ensure a smooth and successful transition for our service members and families. Why? For one, it is the right thing to do, but it is also smart business. These are the people that will encourage their sons, daughters, friends and family to join the military...or not. Best to send them on their way with a good taste in their mouth and a positive story about their experience. This process, the transition assistance program, has seen some improvements over the years, but still needs much work. The program still mostly excludes the family and after all they are transitioning too. I believe that we need to make the transition process mostly virtual and on demand. That way families can gather around the table and participate in the decisions that must be made, like going to school or starting a career, returning to your hometown or going someplace different, remaining with the reserves or separating completely from the military. These are important and oftentimes one-shot opportunities that deserve serious family review. Let's give them the opportunity to make these serious decisions as a family.

Let's also not kick our service members out the door and into the cold, without a support mechanism. Since the mid-2000s, we have experienced a sharp increase in military and veteran suicides. As I previously explained, much of this is due to PTSD and TBI, but it is also a result of our endless wars and the toll they have taken, as well as a veteran support system that is broken. As I mentioned, we have made some improvements to the transition assistance program, but those improvements have all been before the final separation, or what we often refer to as the left side of the 214. The DD214 is the final separation document that provides a service member with important information about their service career and is used for a variety of benefits and proof of service after separation. The problem with our current system is that little attention has been paid to the what happens the day, weeks and months after a service member takes off the uniform.

I introduced a concept that I strongly believe will help military members and families make the transition more successfully. I also believe this will reduce the homelessness and rising number of suicides that we are experiencing among our veterans. No matter how much work we do before a service member transitions or separates from the military, there is still a light switch event that occurs. One day you are in uniform, the next day you are not. One day you can easily enter the base, the next day you cannot. One day you are with your military buddies, the next day you are not. We cannot fully understand what goes through everyone's mind on this day and the days that follow, but as a veteran I can tell you that there is a sense of loss and confusion. The euphoria of getting away from the structure of military life and taking a vacation soon wears off. Then the reality of those decisions that you made in the transition process now take hold. Did you secure a job, or do you need to look for one? Do you have a home to go to? Is the plan to try to reconnect with your old high school friends, or have they moved on?

These issues and the new reality weigh heavily in the days and weeks that follow the light switch event, but they do not have to be faced alone. I believe that instead of receiving your DD214 on your last day of service, you should be required to set an appointment with the local national guard armory or reserve center in your new city of residence. This will serve two important purposes. One, it will give the local military representative, normally a personnel NCO or officer, the opportunity to visit with you and conduct a health and welfare assessment to see how you are doing after separation. This is critical to interrupting any cycles that may lead to depression and suicide. It also provides the local resources to help with finding housing or maybe a job. Remember that national guard and reserve personnel have civilian jobs as well, and often they are senior members of the community. Who better to help you with finding a job than the local military commander that is also a senior VP at the local bank or on the Chamber of Commerce?

Second is the reconnection with military buddies. This is also very important. For most of us, we spent years with our military buddies, and they were our family. Losing that connection can be as difficult as separating from your real family. By linking with military people in your own community, it will help lessen some of that pain and stress.

Once this action has occurred and connection has been made, then the new veteran may choose to join the reserve unit and remain in uniform on a part time basis. They may also realize that they are truly ready to move on and may or may not wish to maintain contact. Either way, the decision is made not before a life-changing, light-switch moment, rather after a period of reflection and realization of what is to come. I truly believe that making this a requirement for all separating service members, we will save lives.

Finally, and perhaps the most controversial of the recommendations that I make in this book. I remember a store sign I saw as a young man: You break it, you own it. As someone that recognizes the importance of our military service members, I believe we need to take that perspective as we think about our veterans. The #2 of the defense department is the deputy secretary. This role has evolved throughout administrations, not unlike any "second in command" position. Sometimes it is more managerial and sometimes it is more public-facing. It should, however, be redefined in my view. The deputy secretary of defense should be also assigned or dual-hatted as the secretary of veterans affairs. The problem that we have today with veteran services and healthcare is one that we cannot seem to fix under any administration. Perhaps the time has come for the Department of Defense to play a bigger responsibility role in the care of former service members. This could also resolve many of the issues we have between the DoD and VA regarding military medical and personnel records.

Under my vision, the defense department has some ownership role in the military person from "cradle to grave". From the minute a new recruit joins the military until the moment they're put in the ground and the family has received their benefits. Some might say that this would diminish the cabinet level of the VA, to which I would reply, "Who cares?" If it improves service to veterans, then it should be done. Also, this proposal does not eliminate the VA; it merely dual-hats the secretary as the, or a, deputy secretary of defense. This places the Pentagon squarely in the decision-making process for veterans and hopefully will eliminate much of the finger pointing that occurs today between the two agencies. It also allows for us to leverage the two separate health systems, which might improve care for veterans, while increasing military care and readiness.

All of this would require congressional action and I am sure the politics of it all would turn it into something it isn't and grind it all to a halt. But the simple fact is that if we don't do something the problem is only going to get worse. We owe it to our current and future generations of service members and veterans to take care and take responsibility for our greatest assets to our national security.

Building a Department of Defense that is More Reflective of the Society We Serve

I've addressed the tools to improve our recruitment, retention and separation. Earlier in this book, I talked about the most important element of our military: people. It deserves repeating here. As I have previously mentioned, the human capital enterprise within the DoD is an often-overlooked area, as leaders focus on weapon systems, readiness, training and the broader policy portfolio. However, efforts over the past years, particularly following Secretary Gates' book, which offered a stunning rebuke of the department's undersecretaries of personnel, things have begun to change. However, many issues remain and new ones under this administration have emerged.

The department still recruits the vast majority of service members from six Southeast states. We are now seeing that this continued "fishing from the same pond" will not sustain the force of the future and will continue the trend of a military that is less reflective of the society we serve. As previously mentioned, this disconnect from society also hurts the military in terms of national commitment. With fewer families committed to military engagements, the less stake they have and ultimately the less they care. The safety and security of our military and our nation relies on a broader demographic within our ranks.

In order to find those new ponds and successfully fish from them, we need to employ the new tools I mentioned for recruiting and retaining. We also need to change our thoughts and attitudes about what makes a successful service member. Yes, success is defined by performance in the role, the ability of the recruit to succeed in a particular job. However, success is also reflected in the diversity of the force—its ability to know and appreciate diverse cultures, the people it will likely encounter around the globe. It has been shown many times that diverse organizations are stronger and more resilient. The different perspectives produce better solutions. So again, diversity is not a weakness or some social experiment; it is strength, safety and security.

CHAPTER 10

WHERE DO WE GO FROM HERE?

"YOU CAN'T USE UP CREATIVITY.
THE MORE YOU USE, THE MORE YOU HAVE."

—*MAYA ANGELOU*

America, the beautiful. America, the brutal. One half limitless potential, one half canvas for supernatural displays of cruelty. A people capable of traversing the stars, all while priding ourselves on the capacity to annihilate worlds. These extremes have manifested throughout all our lives, a give-and-take tango perpetually positioned to dance the nation off a cliff. Some blame red America, some blame blue America, but the reality remains: Every triumph and moral travesty spawns directly from a fundamentally human America.

It is in this chaotic cauldron of conflicting instinctual drives that hundreds of millions of individual dreams and nightmares collide, resulting in a bipolar by-product packaged as national policy. Yet, rather than indicate some horrid defect in the soul of our nation, this duality acts as democratic lifeblood. An ebb and flow of ideas that often blossom into steady progress.

During even the most tumultuous times, America tends to resist the rapid onset of ideological extremes. This immunity has largely been thanks to the organic development of potent antibodies.

Although rarely given the credit they are due, these antibodies come in the form of patron saints of patriotism, individuals who are guided by ideals so high that their attainment requires something akin to a profound spiritual awakening.

You don't ascend to this level of patriotism via tweets and bumper stickers, and you won't find it present in the gluttony and explosions of Independence Day. Instead, it spawns from little inspirational seeds that quickly grow to fill your whole heart, compelling you to serve something higher than yourself—whether you like it or not. From the simple truth telling of a candidate for President, knowing that it might cost him the election, to the soldier reaching out a hand of aid to a child of war, or a crowd of black, white and brown faces calling for justice. These are people that shake us to the core.

I have seen devotion firsthand to America's fundamental promise radically transform lives. From fields of war to the

work we did for transgender service members was also rolled back.

There was a lot of progress in the work we did and the ideas I hope we can move forward in the future. We may have left the battle temporarily, but there is much more of the fight left and I, for one, am far from done!

REFERENCES

Benner, Brenda. "The future of the Army has to involve long-distance learning." The NCO Journal. Fall 1997.

https://books.google.com/books?id=a4HfAAAAMAA-J&lpg=RA10-PA20&dq=todd%20a.%20weiler&p-g=RA10-PA20#v=onepage&q=todd%20a.%20weiler&f=-false

Congress.gov. "Nomination: PN1052—Todd A. Weiler—Department of Defense. 114th Congress (2015-2016).

https://www.congress.gov/nomination/114th-congress/1052

Denchak, Melissa. "Paris Climate Agreement: Everything You Need to Know." December 12, 2018. Natural Resources Defense Council.

https://www.nrdc.org/stories/paris-climate-agreement-everything-you-need-know

Forgey, Quint. "Pompeo signals impending action against ICC for investigating alleged U.S. war crimes." Politico. June 1, 2020.

https://www.politico.com/news/2020/06/01/mike-pompeo-icc-investigating-us-war-crimes-293673

Gramer, Robbie, Colum Lynch, and Jack Detsch. "Trump Cuts U.S. Ties with World Health Organization Amid Pandemic." *Foreign Policy*. May 29, 2020.

https://foreignpolicy.com/2020/05/29/trump-pulls-out-of-who-coronavirus-pandemic-global-health-covid-china-beijing-influence-international-institutions-global-health/

Greider, William. "Reagan's Dangerous Game in Nicaragua." *Rolling Stone*. February 12, 1987.

https://www.rollingstone.com/culture/culture-news/reagans-dangerous-game-in-nicaragua-111446/

Howze, Ray. "Gulf War at 25: Desert Storm a milestone for 101st." *Leaf Chronicle*. February 13, 2017.

https://www.theleafchronicle.com/story/news/local/fort-campbell/2016/02/19/gulf-war-25-desert-storm-milestone-101st/80403596/

Kumparak, Greg. "Niantic will soon let small businesses pay to have a Pokémon GO Pokéstop." *Tech Crunch*. November 6, 2019.

https://techcrunch.com/2019/11/06/niantic-will-soon-open-pokemon-gos-sponsored-location-system-to-small-businesses/

Library of Congress. "Creating the United States."

https://www.loc.gov/exhibits/creating-the-united-states/formation-of-political-parties.html

Malala Fund.

https://malala.org/malalas-story

Mansky, Jackie. "Operation Desert Storm Was Not Won by Smart Weaponry Alone." *Smithsonian Magazine.* January 20, 2016.

https://www.smithsonianmag.com/history/operation-desert-storm-was-not-won-smart-weaponry-alone-180957879/

Maucione, Scott. "The story of a gay pride parade and the Defense Department." *Federal News Network.* June 28, 2016.

https://federalnewsnetwork.com/defense/2016/06/story-gay-pride-parade-defense-department/slide/1/

Nasa Earth Observatory. "Shamal Winds Drive Middle East Duststorm." January 25, 2005.

https://earthobservatory.nasa.gov/images/14560/shamal-winds-drive-middle-east-dust-storm

Park, Roffrey. "7 of the Most Inspiring Leadership Stories." Roffrey Park Institute. February 1, 2018.

https://www.roffeypark.com/leadership-and-management/7-inspiring-leadership-stories/

Rothschild, Mike. "The Most Important Military Leaders in World History." March 11, 2020. Ranker.

https://www.ranker.com/list/most-important-military-leaders-in-the-world/mike-rothschild

Statt, Nick. "Pokémon Go never went away — 2019 was its most lucrative year ever." *The Verge*. January 10, 2020.

https://www.theverge.com/2020/1/10/21060877/pokemon-go-record-revenue-2019-niantic-labs-ar-growth

Stein, Jeff. "Gays in the Gulf." *The Washington Post*. November 22, 1992.

https://www.washingtonpost.com/archive/opinions/1992/11/22/gays-in-the-gulf/83526306-4e92-40ea-afa5-3a411c2db4ae/

U.S. Department of Defense.

https://dod.defense.gov

Weiler, Todd. "Southern border crisis—here's how we can reverse it." *The Hill.* June 2, 2019.

https://thehill.com/opinion/immigration/446538-southern-border-crisis-heres-how-we-can-reverse-it

____. "Sometimes we lead, sometimes we follow and that's okay." *The Hill.* September 23, 2016.

https://thehill.com/blogs/congress-blog/civil-rights/297485-sometimes-we-lead-sometimes-we-follow-and-thats-okay

____. "A military reflective of the society we serve." *The Hill.* December 13, 2016.

https://federalnewsnetwork.com/commentary/2016/12/military-reflective-society-serve/

____.

https://www.toddaweiler.com/home

WhiteHouse.gov. "President Donald J. Trump's Efforts to Combat the Crisis at Our Southern Border Are Delivering Results." October 8, 2019.

https://www.whitehouse.gov/briefings-statements/president-donald-j-trumps-efforts-combat-crisis-southern-border-delivering-results/

___. "Remarks by President Trump to the 74th Session of the United Nations General Assembly." September 25, 2019.

https://www.whitehouse.gov/briefings-statements/remarks-president-trump-74th-session-united-nations-general-assembly/

Wong, Curtis. "A Soldier and His Transgender Daughter Demonstrate True Love in Powerful Short Film." *HuffPost*. November 17, 2018.

https://www.huffpost.com/entry/the-real-thing-transgender-film_n_5bef4438e4b07573881e935d

Zurcher, Anthony. "Hillary Clinton emails - what's it all about?" *BBC*. November 6, 2016.

https://www.bbc.com/news/world-us-canada-31806907

ABOUT THE AUTHOR

Todd A. Weiler has served in top Pentagon posts under Presidents Clinton and Obama. Most recently, he was the Assistant Secretary of Defense for Manpower and Reserve Affairs. A national security expert, Weiler specializes in the challenges facing today's military personnel and families. He is an innovative thought leader on issues impacting military and federal civil servants; military family programs; wounded warrior policies and reserve component issues.

Prior to his civilian appointments, Weiler served in the Army as an attack helicopter pilot and is a decorated combat veteran of Desert Shield/Desert Storm. As an accomplished business leader, Weiler brings a unique perspective to the public and private sector as he demonstrates a needed balance of business acumen and public service, or as he says, "altruism with discipline".

Between his time in the military and public service, Weiler started and grew successful private sector businesses. Today, he operates a consulting firm focused on human capital and IT services.

With a career that spans more than 30 years of military, private and public service, Weiler enjoys sharing his successes and failures with audiences around the world. A little-known background footnote, as a radio DJ and stand-up comedian/impersonator, Weiler mixes humor and serious lessons learned to inspire and amuse audiences from university students to C-suite executives and political leaders.

Weiler is a veteran, national security and business leader, and author of numerous articles, interviews and public speeches. *Untamed Equality* is his debut book.

ACKNOWLEDGEMENTS

I could not possibly start anywhere else, except by thanking my husband, Ediberto "Junior". His perseverance is why this book exists. Every time I would write an op-ed or talk about a policy that I believed should be changed, he would say, "You need to write a book." When I was deep into the fight for transgender equality in the military and for children of service members, like Blue, Junior again pushed. After multiple dismissals of "who would want to read anything I wrote" and "I don't even have enough to say", Junior made a list of book chapters that ultimately became the blueprint for *Untamed Equality*. I would never have done this without his inspiration and drive. He motivates and inspires me every day and is the love of my life.

Living in the world of politics is like wanting a life of stress. For those of us that seek and are privileged to do the work of presidents inside their administrations, it also can be extremely rewarding. I want to thank all of those that I have worked with over the years in the Clinton and Obama administrations. I especially thank my best friend, Ron Keohane, who has stood with me through some great moments and hard times over almost 30 years. Few are as committed to the real work of public service as Ron and it has been an honor to work with him and call him friend.

My family consists of so many, the family I was born into and the one that has taken shape around me throughout my life. My brothers, Jeff and Dana "Mitch", and their spouses, Allison and Angel, are a large part of who I am and what I have become. They have seen me at my funniest and at my saddest; my deepest love and gratitude goes to them. My Brazilian family on my husband's side: Ediberto, Alice, Elizabeth, Erika, Eduardo and Fred, they are all a blessing and a realization of what family means in other parts of the world. We miss some of this in the workaholic country we live in. Their love and support have made a huge difference in our lives.

Three important mentions are those that perhaps unknowingly took actions that landed me here. First is Jim Wright, former Speaker of the House. He asked me to perform as part of a fundraiser and afterward connecting me to the Mondale campaign that started it all; no longer with us, but certainly deserving of my thanks. Second is Kelly Craighead who made that so important call in November 1992 telling me to get my butt up to DC. Finally, is former Secretary of the Air Force, Deborah Lee James, who made the call in 2015 that brought me back to the Pentagon.

The man that wrote the foreword to this book is Sean Astin, my friend also of almost 30 years. As an honored Godfather, I am also grateful to the Astin love and hospitality. They have been my respite when I needed them over the years.

Finally, I want to thank the LEADERS that have inspired me. I may no longer be pursuing my dream of becoming President, but if I were, I would want to be like Bill Clinton. No, he is not a perfect human being, but when it comes to LEADERSHIP, there is no one in my lifetime that has done it better. He led a nation from economic disaster into historic economic prosperity. He took a world toward democracy in a post-Cold War environment by taking the harder right, than the easier wrong. Hillary, as you have read, is a Shero of mine. She is perhaps the most relevant connection I have to national leadership. I have been honored to serve with her since 1992. And as I mentioned in this book, Hillary placed her trust in me with their daughter...an honor that goes beyond any meeting, mention or political appointment. Our world and country would be in a much better place had the will of the American people been followed in 2016 and Hillary Clinton had become President of the United States. Instead, she will take her honored place as a true LEADER for our nation. I mentioned my political hero, Walter Mondale, the first major party candidate to select a woman as a running mate, Geraldine Ferraro. In that 1984 Democratic Party Convention, he took the path of truth...an honorable path that earns historical acclaim, but does nothing in the moment except garner the respect of many young people, like me looking for a LEADER to emulate.